D1564228

The wisdom teachings of a great spiritual master come to life.

"Tanya offers a map of the spiritual landscape, as well as a series of practices for traversing it that, with some tweaking, can be understood and practiced by ordinary spiritual seekers of any religious background. My goal in writing this book is … to make the essential teachings of *Tanya* accessible to as many people as possible." —from the Preface

Sky Light Illuminations

Offers today's spiritual seeker an enjoyable entry into the great classic texts of the world's spiritual traditions. Each classic is presented in an accessible translation, with facing pages of guided commentary from experts, offering readers the keys they need to understand the history, context, and meaning of the text. The series enables readers of all backgrounds to experience and understand classic spiritual texts directly, and to make them a part of their lives.

Also Available in the SkyLight Illuminations Series

Zohar
Annotated & Explained

**Translation and Annotation by
    Daniel C. Matt**
**Foreword by
    Andrew Harvey**

Explains references and mystical symbols in the canonical text of Kabbalah and clarifies its bold claim: We have always been taught that we need God, but in order to manifest in the world, God needs us.

5½ x 8½, 176 pp, Quality PB
978-1-893361-51-5

Hasidic Tales
Annotated & Explained

**Translation and Annotation by
    Rabbi Rami Shapiro**
**Foreword by
    Andrew Harvey**

Demonstrates the spiritual power of unabashed joy, offers lessons for leading a holy life and reminds you that the Divine can be found in the everyday.

5½ x 8½, 240 pp, Quality PB
978-1-893361-86-7

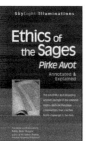

Ethics of the Sages
Pirke Avot—*Annotated & Explained*

**Translation and Annotation by
    Rabbi Rami Shapiro**

Clarifies the ethical teachings of the early Rabbis and highlights parallels with other faith traditions. This is not a book about ethics but a practical guide to living ethically.

5½ x 8½, 192 pp, Quality PB
978-1-59473-207-2

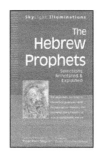

The Hebrew Prophets
Selections Annotated & Explained

**Translation and Annotation by
    Rabbi Rami Shapiro**
**Foreword by Zalman M.
    Schachter-Shalomi (z"l)**

Focuses on the central themes covered by all the prophets: moving from ignorance to wisdom, injustice to justice, cruelty to compassion and despair to joy.

5½ x 8½, 224 pp, Quality PB
978-1-59473-037-5

**For more information about these and other
SkyLight Paths and Jewish Lights books, please visit us at
www.skylightpaths.com and www.jewishlights.com.**

Rabbi Rami Shapiro, a renowned spiritual teacher, is an award-winning storyteller, poet and essayist. He is the author of *The Sacred Art of Lovingkindness: Preparing to Practice; The Divine Feminine in Biblical Wisdom Literature: Selections Annotated & Explained; Ethics of the Sages:* Pirke Avot—*Annotated & Explained; Hasidic Tales: Annotated & Explained; The Hebrew Prophets: Selections Annotated & Explained* (all SkyLight Paths), *Amazing* Chesed: *Living a Grace-Filled Judaism* (Jewish Lights) and other books.

Rabbi Zalman M. Schachter-Shalomi *(z"l)*, the founder of Jewish Renewal and an innovative leader in ecumenical dialogue, authored many books and articles, including *First Steps to a New Jewish Spirit: Reb Zalman's Guide to Recapturing the Intimacy and Ecstasy in Your Relationship with God; Davening: A Guide to Meaningful Jewish Prayer,* winner of the National Jewish Book Award, and *Jewish with Feeling: A Guide to Meaningful Jewish Practice* (all Jewish Lights).

Praise for Rabbi Rami Shapiro's Work

"One of the outstanding leaders in the field of modern spirituality…. His mastery of English and Hebrew enables him to render the ancient words in ways that bring light and inspiration."
—***Jewish Media Review***

"Rami Shapiro has given us two gifts, an illuminating contemporary rendering of this timeless spiritual classic, along with commentary of everyday, personal stories that reveal the joy-filled wisdom. I loved it!"
—**Sylvia Boorstein,** author of *That's Funny, You Don't Look Buddhist*

Also by Rabbi Rami Shapiro

Amazing Chesed
Living a Grace-Filled Judaism

Draws from ancient and contemporary, traditional and non-traditional Jewish wisdom. Reclaims grace as a core Jewish idea.
6 x 9, 176 pp, Quality PB, 978-1-58023-624-9

The Sacred Art of Lovingkindness
Preparing to Practice

Explores Judaism's Thirteen Attributes of Lovingkindness as the framework for cultivating a life of goodness. Shapiro translates these attributes into practices—drawn from the teachings of a variety of faith traditions—that allow you to actualize God's glory through personal deeds of lovingkindness. With a foreword by Marcia Ford.
5½ x 8½, 176 pp, Quality PB, 978-1-59473-151-8

Tanya, the Masterpiece of Hasidic Wisdom

Selected Books in the
SkyLight Illuminations Series

Tanya, the Masterpiece of Hasidic Wisdom

Selections
Annotated & Explained

Translation & annotation by Rabbi Rami Shapiro

Foreword by Rabbi Zalman M. Schachter-Shalomi

For People of All Faiths, All Backgrounds
JEWISH LIGHTS Publishing

Walking Together, Finding the Way ®
SKYLIGHT PATHS ®
PUBLISHING

Tanya, the Masterpiece of Hasidic Wisdom: Selections Annotated & Explained
2014 Quality Paperback Edition

Library of Congress Cataloging-in-Publication Data
Shneur Zalman, of Lyady, 174–1813.
[Likute amarim. English. Selections]
Tanya, the masterpiece of Hasidic wisdom : selections annotated & explained / translation & annotation by Rami Shapiro ; foreword by Zalman M. Schachter-Shalomi. –2010 quality paperback ed.
p. cm. — (Skylight illuminations series)
Includes bibliographical references and index.
ISBN 978-1-59473-275-1 (quality pbk. original : alk. paper) 1. Shneur Zalman, of Lyady, 1745-1813. Likute amarim. 2. Hasidism. 3. Habad. I. Shapiro, Rami M. II. Title.
BM198.2.S56213 2010   2009054330
296.8'332—dc22

ISBN 978-1-59473-359-8 (eBook)

Manufactured in the United States of America
Cover design: Walter C. Bumford III
Cover art: © istockphoto.com / peter zelei

SkyLight Paths Publishing is creating a place where people of different spiritual traditions come together for challenge and inspiration, a place where we can help each other understand the mystery that lies at the heart of our existence.

SkyLight Paths sees both believers and seekers as a community that increasingly transcends traditional boundaries of religion and denomination—people wanting to learn from each other, *walking together, finding the way.*

SkyLight Paths, "Walking Together, Finding the Way," and colophon are trademarks of LongHill Partners, Inc., registered in the U.S. Patent and Trademark Office.

Walking Together, Finding the Way®
Published by SkyLight Paths Publishing / Jewish Lights Publishing
An imprint of Turner Publishing Company
www.skylightpaths.com   www.jewishlights.com

ISBN 978-1-68336-326-2 (hc)

Contents ☐

Foreword □

Rabbi Zalman M. Schachter-Shalomi

Many a Jewish person has said that if it hadn't been for *Tanya* they would not have been able to remain committed to our tradition. This is also true for me. This is why I'm so delighted that Rabbi Rami Shapiro has prepared this rendition of the book. There is much in the book, even in the Chabad authorized translation of *Tanya*, that is inspiring. Yet without filtering and rendering some of the material, the raw content as it stands may be off-putting for some people. What Rami brings to the task is an integral, dare I say it, Taoist lens, an approach that he has used in some of his other brilliant renditions of classical Jewish texts.

For me, too, *Tanya* was the faith saver, a spiritual lifesaver. What I intuited inside its pages I could not find in the schools or synagogues I attended as I grew up in Vienna, Austria. After the Anschluss my family and I crossed the border illegally to Belgium where I met some people who were students of *Tanya*. When I sat with them, singing and praying, I was able to attune to their contemplative and feeling space, which afforded me a sense of signification that nourished a longing for the light that I experienced.

Later on, when I was doing my graduate work in pastoral psychology and psychology of religion, I was able to appreciate what the psychological contributions made by Reb Schneur Zalman and *Tanya* were all about.

The most far-reaching psychological contribution Rabbi Schneur Zalman made was his concept of the *beinoni*. The word itself is as difficult to translate as is the concept. Some translators define it as "average person," but this rendering is a sociological fiction. Rabbi Schneur Zalman intended no such meaning. He understood *beinoni* as a term for the individual who straddled somewhere between *tzaddik* (saint) and *rasha* (wicked person). He therefore begins his teaching by defining *tzaddik* and *rasha*.

Tzaddik

Rabbi Schneur Zalman was of the opinion that *tzaddik* was a qualitative term, not a behavioral one. Were it only behavioral, *tzaddik* would merely have meant someone who behaves righteously more often than not, and, at the deepest level, might sometimes also desire that which is not of God's will. He therefore spoke of "absolute *tzaddik*" and "conditional *tzaddik*." He treats *rasha*, which we will explain later, in the same manner.

The absolute *tzaddik*, in the qualitative sense, is a person who has completely mortified her or his demons so that there is not even so much as an unconscious inclination to invest energy—libido—toward evil. The absolute *tzaddik* cannot even attempt such an inclination since all fascination for evil has been canceled. The *tzaddik*'s disdain for evil, however, is not at all fanatical as it is quiet and existential.

The conditional *tzaddik*, however, while not involved behaviorally in evil or inclined to invest libido toward it in any way, is nonetheless vulnerable to the potential for evil. There may be abhorrence for evil, but it is not absolute, and the fascination for it still lingers on at some unconscious plateau.

Yet, in both categories of *tzaddik*, the vital and decisive principle is the Divine Soul *(Nefesh HaEloki)*, which shares a common ontology with God. Thus, as a *tzaddik* a person could not act against God for it would be tantamount to acting against a person's own nature.

Rasha

The absolute *rasha* is totally under the governance of body drives and emotional whims. Such an individual identifies with the Animal Soul *(Nefesh HaBehamit)*, is one with its will, and, not being reason-directed, completely blocks out any awareness of the manifestation of Divine Soul. The absolute *rasha*, however, is in a rare minority. More common is the conditional *rasha*, driven by impulse, rationalizing but not quite rational, and conforming to pressures from both within and without—characteristics with which most of us can easily identify. We use reason as a tool for furthering the animal dimension of our nature, yet delegate no control to reason over our emotions. We may, for example, be aroused to *teshuvah* (repentance), Torah study, and the performance of *mitzvot* (sacred commandments), but not on a primary level. At best, we may be involved in these peripherally, momentarily enveloped in the holiness they vibrate, but as we step back into our *rasha* condition, all of this disappears like an illusion, though some traces of the experience remain at some level, and once again the Animal Soul is control.

Beinoni

Finally, there is the *beinoni,* the person whose character figures somewhere in between *tzaddik* and *rasha.* The *beinoni* has not sinned behaviorally, but neither has the *beinoni* purged him or herself from evil. And though the *beinoni*'s evil inclinations may fade out during such ecstatic experiences as prayer and the celebration of sacred festivals, eventually they fade in again and become restored to their original strength.

Not too many people are of the category of *beinoni*. To remain a *beinoni* a person has to be able to keep repeating the decision that entails the recognition of the ontological definition of sin as idolatry. A *beinoni* can therefore never act out in sin, for each sin would be akin to idolatry in that, at the very moment the sin is committed, all of a person's energies draw from the evil energy system of *kelipah,* the shell, rather than from the pure source of God. The *beinoni,* recognizing this, makes a conscious and deliberate decision never to draw life energies from any source other than God, a decision which must thereafter be constantly nurtured and reinforced, often at great emotional expense. While it is a difficult, impossible seeming feat, it can be accomplished.

The Psychology of *Beinoni*

At some point, every person needs to make a decision about his or her nature. This philosophical as well as theological homework needs to be done, and it needs to be done consciously. In the process, however, it is often images of self as painted by others, such as roles which others have forced upon you, that become unconsciously interwoven in your self identity. Consequently, you might be innocently inclined to direct your energies toward the fulfillment of these interjected roles. Nonetheless, the overall image you maintain of yourself forms an essential identification. You may decide, for example, that you are essentially an animal, a part of the animal continuum (the lioness, too, loves her cubs, etc.). By dint of this identity option you are a reasoning animal, your rationale perhaps serving as a vehicle for the enhancement of your animal behavior. Once you have chosen this nature, however, you cannot expect to transcend the animal continuum, and you would not have any reason to do so.

On the other hand, you might opt to image yourself as a divine child, in which case you perceive your body as an instrument for life divine. Before the advent of Hasidism, this was the only available alternative for the *tzaddik*. Only by an heroic exertion of will and with the help of God were a select few able to reach this level. Others continued to fluctuate between the Animal and the Divine. Still others (i.e., the followers of Shabbatai Zvi, the seventeenth-century Jewish mystic who claimed to be the long-awaited messiah, and later converted to Islam) identified the Divine and Animal Souls as one and the same, and combined them both into a single antinomian heave, hoping to thereby avoid the strain of the constant struggles between the two. But, as was borne out by history, such an attempt at antinomian monism resulted in a demonic fiasco.

The Rational Soul

Rabbi Schneur Zalman proposed a fourth option: The human being, he taught, is Reason. Indeed, our primary soul, the arena of our life force, is the Rational Soul *(Nefesh HaSikhlit)*, the final arbiter for most of us. The Rational Soul will align itself either with the Divine Soul (and only after much effort and with God's help) or with the Animal Soul (by choice or default). By this system, the will is free, driven neither by animal or divine necessities, and is able to choose to perform the will of God or to transgress it and rebel. Though a person's will is totally free, it is nonetheless contained by reasoning and conceptualizing in order to maintain a beneficial relationship with other people and with the universe.

The difference, then, between the vehicle of Rational Soul and that of Divine Soul is that with the Rational Soul alone a person can only reach the God *idea*, but with the Divine Soul, a person can reach God's Self.

Chabad and Affect

Nonetheless, all of this may indeed have solely philosophical significance were it not for another decisive dimension: The energies of mind, or reason *(mohin)*, influence the affective modes, or emotions *(middot)*. In fact, each emotion *(middah)* is a consequence of an intelligence *(seichel)*, a thought sequence or idea syndrome, consisting of:

1. *Chochmah* (Wisdom): essential and qualitative truth
2. *Binah* (Understanding): truth in relation to other *seichel*
3. *Da'at* (Knowledge): empirical truth

If only *Chochmah* were active in any given *seichel*, the thought would be but a mere abstraction. If only *Binah* were operative, there would be a *how* but no *what*. It is *Da'at* alone which provides the given, the *that*. When I know *what* is, *how* it is, and *that* it is, I am involved in a meaningful situation in which I can act.

On the premise of these concepts, an innovative way of divine service *(avodah)* becomes possible, for we can then meditate on *how* God's goodness operates via divine providence, and that God, out of the pure goodness of the divine nature, acts benevolently toward us. When exercised at the proper depth of consciousness, this meditation will inevitably move us to experience a flow of gratitude toward God. This sense of appreciation issues forth from the Rational Soul, but, moreover, it forms a loving connection between the soul and God since the Divine Soul naturally loves its divine root and source. The resulting experience is one in which divine emotion blends with an *amor dei intellectualis*, an intellectual love of God.

The Vicissitudes of the *Beinoni*

Even by living a life directed by religion, the Animal Soul is still constantly nurtured and reinforced. After all, kosher food, too, is pleasing to the Animal Soul. In a like manner, each time the Animal Soul avoids any form of discomfort or exertion, its resistance becomes strengthened and the "substance (matter) overcomes the form." Anxiety and frustration *(atzvut)*, on the other hand, tend to dull the keenness of the perceptual judgment necessary for the Rational Soul to maintain a steady *beinoni* mode. *Atzvut* evokes self-pity and, consequently, self-indulgence. Next, lethargy may set in ("accedia" is the scholastic term usually given for this malady). The Rational Soul is then no longer able to hold a firm grasp on a meditation, and the Divine Soul suffers a falling of the mind *(nefilat ha'mohin)*, and a dulling of mind and heart *(timtum ha'moah v'ha'lev)*. This form of depression, begotten by the unmitigated anxiety, does not yield to homiletics or meditative exercises.

The Remedy
Here, Rabbi Schneur Zalman suggests some remedial methods that might sound severe and drastic in comparison with the usually rosy hued portrayal of Hasidism by neo-Hasidim. Not given to any illusions, he even goes so far as to disqualify the Baal Shem Tov's method of raising up fallen drives, thoughts, and images, when it comes to salvaging the very delicate mode of *beinoni*. His successor, too, Rabbi Dov Ber of Lubavitch, authored three books on the subject, in which he prescribes a strenuous, painful program of intense penance, beginning with an exacting and austere discipline, for those seeking to reach the optimal heights of prayer.

Rabbi Schneur Zalman suggests that you convert your floating anxiety into objective bitterness and then integrate it into your sinful state. As a *beinoni*, you need to turn all the potential energies of self-destruction toward the service of God. Instead of sulking proudly in your inability to soar toward heaven, and rather than seething with paralyzing frustration and yielding to morose self-pity, you need to turn all these energies against your blocked Animal Soul. Having done that, you must then sever your identification with your Animal Soul and free your Rational Soul from its confinement to it.

Timing, however, is of great importance throughout this process, and all the necessary effort and exertion must not be expended prematurely. You must also weep over your lot of utter poverty and continuous inner struggle. You must become so broken in spirit that your only remaining reason for existing is God's creative and commanding will. Nonetheless, this is your ultimate salvation, for after such uncontrollable weeping, you are renewed by God. Furthermore, the shell is shattered and a fresh joy will now be able to come through and fill you since it becomes thereby clear to you that God desires your service. Your sensitivity, too, is restored and you can again render the decisions which impress the form upon the substance.

Regression is, of course, possible. Rabbi Schneur Zalman counsels the *hasid* to desensitize him- or herself against frustration and anxiety by deliberately inducing these moods now and then through *itkaffia*, the suppression of the *sitra achra* (side of the "otherness"), which is achieved by depriving the Animal Soul of physical organ pleasure or by slowing it down to a less manic pace.

Inner and Outer Reality

Unlike the mind of the average person, terribly splintered in all directions, the mind of the absolute *tzaddik* is divinely unified, and the *tzaddik*'s awareness is never split. In the same manner, the mind of the absolute *rasha* is also whole, a complete animal's tool. The *beinoni*, however, is always caught in the split, always suffering from ambivalence even when making a conscious decision. Judged constantly by both the good and evil inclinations, the *beinoni* is at all times aware of the inner dissent between the two, even when rendering a good choice. When, as a *beinoni*, you choose to love God, for example, you cannot experience that love fully; you can only will it as strongly as is within your power. You are at a further disadvantage as a *beinoni* attempting to love fully because, being primarily self-directed, you are not much of a social creature to begin with.

In the final analysis, the *beinoni* works always with his or her will. But there is, of course, much more to a person than will. Even if you will something, is it true? Is it honest? Is it authentic? Genuine? Saturated with too much experience, the *beinoni* is not free from dissonant dissent and will, only a few moments after asserting the will to love God, experience the full emotional impact of a coarse temptation.

Does this mean, however, that the *beinoni* is a hypocrite? No, says Rabbi Schneur Zalman, because reality is not determined by the meaning put forth by humankind but by the meaning which issues forth from Torah ("The Holy One Blessed Be God looked into the Torah and created the world"). The *beinoni*, then, tunes in to objective transcendental reality, independent of his or her own inauthenticity. In a more profound way, the *beinoni*'s nature is more fully authentic in that it is the very nature of the Divine Soul to offer *all* of herself to God, and that includes the doubts, the ambivalence, the contradictory experiences. Moreover, this ontological underpinning comprises the basis for meditations which can bring about profound emotive results. The question, of course, is, can any person do all this? And to that Rabbi Schneur Zalman responds with a resounding "Yes."

Yes. Taking Jews and Judaism as an example, you need only to arouse your natural love, which is so powerful that a Jew cannot be persuaded or threatened to apostasy. Even the *yetzer hara* (evil inclination) must constantly reckon with this omnipotent love for God and its resulting aggressive preservation of Jewish characteristic and identification which constitutes the very power of Jewish survival. Thus, regardless of how far from the path the modern Jew may have strayed, there is still the affirmation of "I am still a good Jew," or, in the words of *Tanya:* "I am still standing in my Jewishness." Of course, the same could be said of anyone in any tradition—love is key.

In this poetic re-turning to *Tanya*, Rabbi Rami has made it possible to transcend the sociological average and to find the tools to aspire to *beinoni*-hood. As Rabbi Schneur Zalman writes, "The *beinoni*'s mode is the measure of every person. Let everyone aspire to it. For anyone can become a *beinoni* at any time." Rabbi Rami's work makes this all the more doable.

Preface □

This is not your *zayde*'s *Tanya*. In fact, unless your *zayde* (grandfather) was a Hasidic Jew, he most likely never even heard of *Tanya*. Chances are, neither have you. Yet *Tanya* is one of most important articulations of Jewish spirituality ever written. In fact, members of the CHaBaD school of Hasidism, for whom *Tanya* was written, consider the book to be as central to Jewish literacy as Torah, Talmud, and *Zohar*—the Five Books of Moses, the canon of rabbinic law and tradition, and the thirteenth-century mystical commentary on the Bible that formed the foundation for much of Kabbalah (Jewish mysticism).

So why haven't you heard of it?

First, because *Tanya* is rarely taught outside the world of CHaBaD Hasidism, a movement within Orthodox Judaism. Second, even when it is, *Tanya* is so dense and steeped in kabbalistic terminology that most people just cannot follow it. Even when presented by as skilled a teacher, scholar, and mystic as Rabbi Adin Steinsaltz, whose three-volume exploration of *Tanya* is the classic English guide to the text, *Tanya* still remains largely impenetrable to all but the most dedicated students of Jewish mysticism.

Third, *Tanya* was written for Jews who are seeking not simply a relationship with God, but a transformative encounter with the Infinite that will, at least for a moment, empty them of all sense of separate self. To delve into *Tanya* properly, that is to take *Tanya* on as a practice rather than just an exercise in intellectual curiosity, you need a living teacher well versed in biblical, rabbinic, and kabbalistic Judaism, someone deeply familiar with Jewish meditation practices who has experienced the emptying of self and come back from it.

Yet *Tanya* is too rich a teaching to be limited to those few Jews who desire not simply to meet God but also to be annihilated in God. *Tanya* offers a map of the spiritual landscape, as well as a series of practices for traversing it that, with some tweaking, can be understood and practiced by ordinary spiritual seekers of any religious background. Providing that approach to *Tanya* is what this book is all about.

Tanya, the Masterpiece of Hasidic Wisdom is a version of *Tanya* written specifically for those who lack the extensive Jewish education and practical experience of those Jews for whom *Tanya* was originally written. I have selected to translate only the key passages from each of *Tanya*'s fifty-three chapters and have rendered them in as simple and direct a manner as possible, minimizing kabbalistic jargon and highlighting the universal aspects of the text. In addition, I have chosen to present the text as free verse rather than straight prose, because I find it is easier for readers to grasp the message of *Tanya* when presented in short lines as opposed to blocks of dense text. For readers interested in comparing my creative rendering with the original Hebrew or official English translation, I have provided page references to *The Tanya: Bi-Lingual Edition*, published by Kehot Publication Society in 1998. It is referenced throughout this book as "Kehot edition."

Still, there is no denying that *Tanya* is a Jewish text, and I have done nothing to weaken that fact. What I have done, and I hope have done successfully, is render the Judaism of *Tanya* accessible to everyone.

My goal in writing this book is twofold: first, to make the essential teachings of *Tanya* accessible to as many people as possible, and, second, to encourage those readers who find my simplified *Tanya* exciting to seek out a teacher and delve into the original.

As always, I am greatly indebted to Emily Wichland, my editor at SkyLight Paths, for guiding me in making this version of *Tanya* clear, concise, and compelling. Emily is an author's dream: an editor who edits with the reader in mind. If my selections and renditions of *Tanya* speak to you and deepen your sense of God's presence in, with, and as all things, we both have Emily to thank.

Introduction ☐

I'm always talking about God. In fact, I confess to spending more time talking about God than I do talking with God. I find the topic of God infinitely fascinating. Ten or so years ago I was invited to a dinner party
specifically devoted to God talk. When the conversation turned to Judaism,
I laid out as concisely as I could the major ideas found in this book:

1. The nonduality of God, and the realization that God is all that is
2. That God's nonduality necessitates duality, and the recognition of
   the One and the many as different "sides" of the nondual God
3. The five dimensions of reality and their corresponding intelligences
   (body, heart, mind, soul, and spirit), and how all are present in each
   of us
4. The purpose of *mitzvot*, the practices of Jewish life, as catalysts to
   God realization and the hallowing of all life through godliness

When we broke for a moment to get dessert, one of the guests, a disciple of Ramana Maharshi, one of the greatest Hindu saints of the twen-
tieth century, cornered me in the kitchen, and said, "Rabbi, I have been
a Jew all my life, and I never heard any of the ideas you were talking
about. I mean it sounded like Hinduism—everything is God! I have to
know, is this your personal take on Judaism, or did you learn this from
authentic Jewish sources?"

"Everything I said tonight," I said, "and everything I find compelling
within Jewish spirituality comes from one book. It's called *Tanya*, after
the opening word of the text, 'It was taught,' and it was written more
than two hundred years ago by Rabbi Schneur Zalman of Liadi, the
founder of CHaBaD[1] Hasidism, known to his followers as the Alter Rebbe,
or the Old Master."

"Never heard of it! Is it available in English? Where can I get a copy? I have to get a copy!"

I wasn't surprised that he hadn't heard of the book, for it is little known, let alone read, outside the world of CHaBaD, a movement of Orthodox Judaism. Yet the book is readily available in a bilingual Hebrew/English edition from Kehot Publication Society, the publishing arm of the CHaBaD movement in Brooklyn, New York. I suggested he order a copy and gave him my e-mail address so he could let me know what he thought of the book if he did indeed read it.

I got that e-mail less than three months later. While I didn't save it, and cannot quote it verbatim, the gist of the e-mail went like this:

> Dear Rabbi Rami,
> What the hell is this book talking about? I cannot make any sense of it at all. I know you said it was a central part of your learning and teaching, but for the life of me I can't see how. I have never read anything so dense in all my life. I'm glad you find something in it, but I think I will stick with Ramana. I knew there was a reason I left Judaism. It just doesn't speak to me.

For a moment I was surprised that this clearly intelligent and spiritually well-versed adult couldn't understand what it was the Alter Rebbe was saying in *Tanya*. Then I was saddened that I had failed to reach a fellow Jew with the wisdom of Judaism. And then I was chagrined that I had urged upon a novice a book that was written for Hasidim (very pious and often mystically inclined Orthodox Jews) steeped in the vocabulary of classical and mystical Judaism. What was I thinking? Or was I thinking at all? I had spent years studying *Tanya* and still approach it with the utmost trepidation, knowing that I am but gleaning from the far corners of the Alter Rebbe's insights, and here I passed it on as if it were an introductory text.

I e-mailed my apologies and offered to answer as best I could any questions the book raised, but I never got a reply. This encounter, however, left me with a deep desire to provide readers with a way into *Tanya* that honored the text even as it tried to make it accessible to those the Alter Rebbe never imagined addressing. After a number of fitful starts, the result is the book you now hold in your hands.

Tanya, the Masterpiece of Hasidic Wisdom: Selections Annotated and Explained is a doorway into the original text. My aim in writing this book is to provide you with a version of *Tanya* that, while true to the original, is written in contemporary English designed to minimize the need for formal Jewish and kabbalistic training; a version that will get the essential ideas of *Tanya* out to a broader readership—spiritual seekers of all faiths and none—who are open to the wisdom of sages regardless of the tradition from which they hail.

Tanya was intended for Rabbi Schneur Zalman's nineteenth-century Hasidim and hence presupposes a level of kabbalistic knowledge most of us lack. While I have done my best to choose sections from *Tanya* that are accessible to a wider audience, it is impossible to work with the text without having some sense of the philosophical and spiritual framework on which the book is based. What I have done in this book is present these ideas as I understand them, and as I find them to be of value to others, rather than as officially sanctioned by CHaBaD Hasidism itself.

This is, admittedly, a radical position to take, and some readers and critics may take issue with it. After all, why not simply explain the text as other Hasidic teachers have and continue to do? Why try to make it relevant to people outside the Hasidic world?

My response to this is simple: first, there are a number of books, websites, and even video-blogs that seek to expound *Tanya* within the CHaBaD framework, and I see no reason to add yet another; second, I am a student of *Tanya* and not a follower of CHaBaD Hasidism, and have no authority to speak for that movement; and, third, keeping *Tanya* "in house" denies the wider world of spiritual seekers even a glimpse into the Alter Rebbe's spiritual genius.

We live in an age of interspiritual exploration, and tens of millions of spiritual seekers are no longer satisfied with confining themselves to one religion only. These people have a deep hunger for spiritual wisdom regardless of the tradition from which it comes. And it is to these people that I offer this book.

My assumption in writing this book, then, is not simply that most readers are not well educated Jewishly and kabbalistically, but that in fact many readers are not Jews. Many readers of this book are spiritual seekers with varying degrees of education and training in various religious traditions but are not, and have no intention of becoming, Jewish, Hasidic, or practitioners of Kabbalah to the extent that the Alter Rebbe assumed his students already were.

Given this assumption and my goal of making parts of *Tanya* accessible to a wider audience, I have translated the text freely and in a manner that speaks to those for whom this book is intended. This does not mean I have misrepresented *Tanya*, only that I have sought to present the ideas of the book in as accessible a manner as possible. Let me be more specific.

While the focus of the Alter Rebbe is on Jews alone, I have widened that focus and applied what the Rebbe has to say to all human beings.

While *Tanya* is written for the Rebbe's students, all of whom were men, I have adapted the language of my version of the material to be more inclusive. To avoid the limitations of gendered pronouns, I have cast the text as a direct address to the reader, speaking of "you" and "your," rather than "he" and "his."

What I have provided in this selected reading of *Tanya* are the key spiritual ideas addressed in the text. In so doing, I have avoided secondary material that would require extensive background in biblical, rabbinic, and kabbalistic thinking. In this way, this selection offers you a solid introduction to the full *Tanya*, allowing you to identify the core teachings without being overwhelmed or distracted by supportive material.

My commentary on *Tanya* presents the kabbalistic ideas of the text in a universalist manner; that is, I have presented the teachings of the Alter Rebbe in the light of my own understanding of and spiritual training in Judaism, Buddhism, Hinduism, and the field of comparative religion.

While I have made no attempt to compare and contrast the Alter Rebbe's teaching to similar teachings found in different traditions, my understanding of *Tanya* cannot help but reflect my training in many different religious traditions.

Indeed, this is the underlying aim of this book: to present teachings from a deeply Jewish text to people who, though not among its intended audience, can and will nonetheless benefit from reading it.

What Is *Tanya*?

Tanya, so-called after the opening word of the text, *tanya* ("it was taught"), was written by Rabbi Schneur Zalman of Liadi over a twenty-year period beginning in 1771 or 1772 and published in book form in 1797. Originally titled *Likkutei Amarim* ("Collection of Discourses and Teachings") and subtitled *Sefer shel Beinonim* ("Book for the Inbetween-ers"), *Tanya* is a guide for those who seek to attain the spiritual degree of *beinoni*, a person who, while still attached to the body and bodily passions, drives, and even obsessions, has yet learned to master these by continually concentrating mind and heart on the infinite spaciousness of *Ayn Sof*, the nondual Godhead.

Rabbi Schneur Zalman is also the founder of CHaBaD Hasidism, and among his followers *Tanya* is called *Torah Shebeksav shel Chassidus CHaBaD*, "The Written Torah of CHaBaD Hasidism." This is not meant as hyperbole, for the followers of CHaBaD believe that *Tanya* should be ranked just below the Hebrew Bible as a seminal work of divine revelation and that all future developments in Hasidic thought can be found in *Tanya* itself.[2]

Originally delivered orally over the course of several years, Rabbi Schneur Zalman decided to publish chapters of the book in manuscript form and urged his followers to copy them. The material was released in three stages, beginning with chapters 1–30 in 1792, followed a bit later by chapters 31–44, and then by the closing chapters, 45–51. Each chapter appeared in its own pamphlet (*kuntreis*), and the collection was referred to as the *Sefer HaEitzos*, "The Book of Advice."

Within two years of this decentralized copying process, the Rebbe began to receive letters from readers asking for further clarification regarding various passages found in the many pamphlets. From the letters it became clear that copyists were introducing errors into the text. Thinking these errors to be minor and inadvertent, the Rebbe took no action. By 1795, however, it became clear to him that many among those who opposed the Rebbe's teaching and Hasidism in general were deliberately falsifying *Tanya* chapters to alter the Rebbe's teachings and to discredit Hasidic thought. To correct the errors and protect the teachings, the Rebbe authorized the publication of *Tanya* as a complete book, using the opportunity to edit and revise the text and add two additional chapters to the original fifty-one.

In 1796 the Rebbe chose the printing house of Reb Moshe Shapiro in Slavita, Russia, to print the text, trusting Reb Shapiro to reproduce the text exactly as he received it. The first two hundred copies of *Tanya* were completed on December 20, 1796, and delivered to the Rebbe a week later, on the second day of Hanukkah. To date, *Tanya* has undergone more than five thousand printings.

Up until 1958 all of these editions were in the original Hebrew only, limiting the outreach of the text to those who could read Hebrew. To broaden its readership, the text was translated into Yiddish in 1958, and four years later into English. Today, *Tanya* is available in many languages, including French, German, Italian, Spanish, Russian, Portuguese, Arabic, and Braille.

Tanya comprises fifty-three transcribed talks of Rabbi Schneur Zalman, the Alter Rebbe. The core of *Tanya* is a close examination of a single verse of Torah: "For this thing is very near to you, in your mouth and in your heart, that you may do it" (Deuteronomy 30:14).

"This thing" refers to the *mitzvot*, the divine commandments or spiritual practices of Judaism that, when done with the proper intention (*kavanah*), can generate a love and awe of God so intense as to awaken you to the knowledge of your unity with God (*da'at devekut*), the realization that you are an extension of God the way a ray of sunlight is an extension of the sun.

"Very near" refers to the fact that union with God is not a special state you must achieve, but an already extant reality to which you must awaken. God is All in all. There is nothing that is not God. You do not have to bridge the gap between yourself and God; you only have to see that there is no gap at all. The purpose of doing *mitzvot* is to reveal that truth. *Mitzvot* accomplish this task by releasing in you the love and awe needed to awaken you to the fact of your inseparability from God. Love and awe are *very near to you*; they already exist in you, and all you have to do is release them. You do not have to generate these feelings as much as surrender to them. Spiritual awakening is not a matter of creating a new situation, but of returning (*teshuvah*) to your original state.

Who Was Rabbi Schneur Zalman of Liadi?

Born in 1745 in Liozna, a tiny village in Belarus, Schneur Zalman was a Torah prodigy who, under the tutelage of Rabbi Issachar Ber of Lubavitch, had mastered both Torah and Talmud by the time of bar mitzvah (thirteen years of age). Two years later he married Sterna Segal, the daughter of a wealthy businessman who saw to it that his new son-in-law would be financially free to pursue his studies without the burden of having to earn a living.

Rabbi Zalman's interests were not restricted to Talmudic law, and he studied mathematics, geometry, and astronomy, along with the more esoteric discipline of Lurianic Kabbalah. In 1764 he became a disciple (*hasid*) of Rabbi Dovber of Mezeritch, a member of the inner circle of rabbis who followed Rabbi Israel ben Eliezer, known as the Baal Shem Tov, the founder of Hasidism.

Lurianic Kabbalah is named after its creator, Rabbi Isaac Luria (1534–72), called the Ari (Lion), an acronym for *Elohai Rabbi Yitzchak*, "the Divine Rabbi Isaac." According to the Ari, prior to creation the Infinite Godhead (*Ayn Sof*) filled all space. In order to make room for creation, the Infinite Godhead contracted, leaving room at the center, in which creation was to take place. The act of contraction is called *tzimtzum*.

Having created space, God sought to reenter that space through ten vessels (*kelim*) called *sefirot* (numbers), designed to hold divine light in different concentrations, allowing for the myriad forms of life to arise. While all things were in fact variations of the One Thing, they would have a sense of selfhood and independence that would allow them to function autonomously while yet forming an interdependent whole.

The reentry of God into space was accomplished in four gradations:

Assiyah, the emergence of the physical world as form
Yetzirah, the formation of ideal forms
Beriah, the capacity of light to create form
Atzilut, the emanation of pure light

All four originated in a fifth level, called *Adam Kadmon*, the primordial selfhood of God.

If creation had gone as planned, all five worlds would function flawlessly. Unfortunately, nothing went as planned. The vessels (*kelim*) designed to hold the inpouring of God's light shattered, and the light of God spilled madly through the space created by God's contraction. Sparks of God's light became trapped in shards of broken vessels and, so to speak, became alienated from their Source. According to Rabbi Luria, the task of the Jew is to seek out the trapped sparks of God and liberate them by hallowing the physical world through adherence to the *mitzvot*, the 613 sacred commandments or spiritual practices revealed by God in Torah.

While it may be true that the Ari meant us to take his cosmology literally, it is also true that the Alter Rebbe did not. The idea that God could be alienated from anything, especially God's own self, was anathema to him. Rather than reject the ideas of the Ari, the Alter Rebbe reframed them from a psychospiritual perspective. God is not fragmented; humans are fragmented. God is not broken; humans are broken. God isn't trapped in the physical world; God is hiding as the physical world so that we who inhabit that world can find God and end our own fragmentation and brokenness by realizing we are one with all in, with, and as God.

By 1788 Rabbi Zalman had become the leader of the Hasidic movement in Lithuania, a major center of anti-Hasidic sentiment among Jews. The opponents of Hasidism, whom the Hasidim called Adversaries (*Misnagdim*), issued a *cherem,* or ban, against the Hasidim, but despite organized Jewish opposition, the Alter Rebbe established a strong network of Hasidic centers throughout the region.

The Alter Rebbe was a supporter of the tzarist leadership in Russia, yet despite this, Orthodox Jewish leaders opposed to Rabbi Schneur Zalman and his teachings managed to have him arrested by the Russian authorities in 1798 and tried for treason. Their plan was to convince the court that the Rebbe's efforts to raise money for impoverished Jews living in the Ottoman Empire was in fact a ruse to cover up anti-Russian scheming with the Turks. The Alter Rebbe was taken to St. Petersburg and imprisoned in the Petropavlovski prison for fifty-three days. Examined by a secret commission, he was released later that year.

Two years later, he was again arrested and imprisoned in St. Petersburg, but his release was secured after only a few weeks. Although the conditions of his release prohibited him from leaving St. Petersburg, the new tzar, Alexander I, overturned the ruling and announced that the rabbi was free to teach his doctrines without restriction.

Upon his release, Rabbi Zalman, at the invitation of Prince Stanislaw Lubomirski of Liadi, moved to Liadi and made the town his headquarters. From there he began to expand his network of Hasidim and spread his teaching.

In 1812 Napoleon's army invaded Russia. Most Jewish leaders supported or at least remained silent regarding the Napoleonic invasion. Jewish life under Tzar Alexander was harsh and precarious, while Napoleon offered Jews (at least as individuals if not as a people) freedom and safety. The Alter Rebbe, however, actively opposed the invasion and supported the tzar. His reasoning, articulated in a letter to his friend Rabbi Moshe Meizeles, is revealing:

> Should Napoleon be victorious, wealth among the Jews will be abundant ... but the hearts of Israel will be separated and distant from their Father in heaven. But if our master Alexander will triumph, though poverty will be abundant ... the heart of Israel will be bound and joined with their Father in Heaven ... And for God's sake: Burn this letter![3]

Schneur Zalman anticipated what in fact came to pass: as Jews found freedom and financial success in Western capitalism, their loyalty to traditional Judaism and matters of the spirit declined. But there may be more to the Alter Rebbe's concerns than the allures of material wealth. Napoleon established his own Sanhedrin, or rabbinic court, made up of Jews loyal to him, and positioned himself as the long-awaited Messiah, pretending even to have conquered the Holy Land. Aware of the damage false messianic claims have caused Jews in the past, the Alter Rebbe could have feared another blow to the Jewish spiritual psyche when this new French messiah failed to live up to his promises.

Whatever his reasoning, the Alter Rebbe was no friend of the invaders and died while fleeing the French army in 1813. The Alter Rebbe's son, Dov Baer, became the second rebbe of CHaBaD Hasidism, and it was he who moved CHaBaD's headquarters from Liadi to Lubavitch, the town from which the movement received its unofficial name, Lubavitcher Hasidism.

The Alter Rebbe's politics and organizational skills aside, it is *Tanya* that will prove to be his most precious gift to the world. Studied daily by tens of thousands of Lubavitcher Hasidim, as well as an ever-increasing number of others outside the Hasidic community, *Tanya* brings a level of mystical insight and spiritual practice rarely found in mainstream Judaism.

What Is CHaBaD Hasidism?

Hasidism is a Jewish revivalist movement founded by Rabbi Israel ben Eliezer (1698–1760), who was called the Besht, an acronym for Baal Shem Tov, "Master of the Good Name." A *baal shem*, "master of the Name," was an itinerant wonderworker who used the Names of God, especially the four-letter Hebrew Name of God—*Yod*, *Hei*, *Vav*, *Hei*, or *YHVH*—in amulets designed to heal the sick, ease the pains of childbirth, and improve the finances of the poor. Most of these *baale shem* (plural) were con artists preying on the hardship of others. Rabbi Israel ben Eliezer was different.

His concern was with healing the spirit and helping Jews realize the presence of God and the joy such realization brought with it. Where most rabbis of his day were devoted to the intellectual pursuit of God, Rabbi Israel was devoted to the heart. Where most rabbis focused on those Jews with the potential for scholarly achievement, Rabbi Israel reached out to the uneducated and simple. It was this concern that earned him the added designation of *tov*, "good."

The Baal Shem Tov's concern with the common folk may have stemmed from his own upbringing. Orphaned and raised as a ward of Okup, his native village in the Carpathian Mountains, Rabbi Israel was thought to be an ignoramus as a child. This was far from the case, but the young Israel preferred to keep his learning a secret. Working as a school attendant, Israel would accompany the children to and from school (*cheder*), teaching them through melody and dance the joy of living in God's presence.

The town's leaders married Rabbi Israel to the sister of Rabbi Abraham Gershon of Kutow. Rabbi Abraham opposed the marriage, arguing that his sister should be wed to a scholar, but he relented and even took the couple to live in his home. It was there that Rabbi Abraham discovered his brother-in-law to be not only a scholar but also a man of great spiritual depth.

In time, a small circle called the "holy company" (*chavurah kaddisha*) gathered around the Baal Shem Tov. This group of sages offered a new understanding of Judaism and Jewish practice rooted not so much in the intellectual acumen of scholars, but in the heartfelt piety of the laity. The Besht, in contrast to his scholarly contemporaries, taught that the realization of a person's union with God was not reserved for the intellectual elite, but was a fact of life open to anyone willing to serve God in joy. Joy, not scholarship, became the hallmark of the emerging movement of Hasidism.

A *hasid* (plural: *hasidim*) is a lover of God and godliness. The word itself comes from *chesed*, "compassion," and Hasidim strive to be people of great charity and kindness. After the death of the Baal Shem Tov, holy companies of Hasidim continued to gather around the members of the Baal Shem Tov's original company. These rabbis were called *rebbes* ("masters"; singular: *rebbe*) or *tzaddikim* ("saints"; singular: *tzaddik*). The rebbe was to model the passionate love of God and godliness and to help his followers achieve it for themselves.

With the passing of the original members of the holy company, their students became rebbes in their own right, and the movement spread rapidly. Rabbi Schneur Zalman was of this generation. Like his colleagues and his teachers, he, too, revered the teachings of the Baal Shem Tov, but unlike many in the movement, the Alter Rebbe also valued the work of the mind.

While in no way seeking to denigrate the emphasis on heart-centered joy and service to God, Rabbi Schneur Zalman began to reclaim the importance of scholarship. He called his understanding of Hasidism by the acronym CHaBaD after three Hebrew terms: *Chochmah*, *Binah*, and *Da'at*—intuitive wisdom, rational understanding, and the integrative knowledge of God's presence in, with, and as all reality that arises from the merger of the two. He believed that these three faculties exist to some degree in all beings, but only human beings have the capacity to develop them to the degree necessary to reveal the fact that all beings are manifestations of the One Being, God, or *Ayn Sof*, the Unbounded Infinite. The goal of CHaBaD is to awaken to the knowledge of God as all reality, and the realization that you are never separate from or even other than God; as our Sages taught, "There is no place devoid of God."[4]

This emphasis on the intellect (*seichel*), and its capacity for intuitive wisdom, rational understanding, and integrative knowledge (*Chochmah*, *Binah, and Da'at*), is one of the distinguishing characteristics of CHaBaD Hasidism. Where other rebbes valued emotion over intellect, Rabbi Schneur Zalman upheld the intellect as supreme, and honored it. Indeed, it is the intellect that has the power to intensify the emotions, rather than the other way around. When your mind truly understands the nonduality of God, you are awake to your intimate union with God, as God, and this triggers an intensity of emotion that brings you to emptying of form (*bittul hayesh*) into the infinite oneness of God.

A second distinguishing element of the Alter Rebbe's teaching was his emphasis on God's nonduality (*shlemut*). While normative Judaism speaks of God in dualistic terms, as if God were other than creation, the Alter Rebbe understood creation as an extension of God, the way sunlight is an extension of the sun. While there is a relative difference between the sun and its rays, in no way can the rays be separated from the sun nor the sun from its rays. Just as the rays of the sun are a natural part of the sun and essential to what it is to be a sun, so creation is a natural part of God and what it means to be God.

As his critics charged, the Alter Rebbe's position was clearly panentheistic. Panentheism is the theological stance affirming that all (*pan*) reality is in (*en*) God (*theos*). Creation is an extension of God just as a wave is an extension of the ocean. And just as waves are nothing without the ocean, so the myriad forms of God visible to us as self and other are nothing without God. The aim of CHaBaD is to realize this nothingness (*Ayn*) in every form (*Yesh*).

CHaBaD's panentheism, however, should not be mistaken for world-denying or in any way denigrating of the body. On the contrary, form (*Yesh*) is no less God than emptiness (*Ayn*). God's nonduality (*shlemut*) does not allow for one or the other and necessitates both. Because the world of form matters, CHaBaD emphasizes keeping the *mitzvot* of Judaism, those spiritual practices designed to reveal the unity of the One and the many. As *Tanya* makes clear, the intellectual understanding of reality gives rise to a quality of physical engagement with reality that unleashes a transformative love for life in all its forms, even as it knows those forms to be temporary expressions of the infinite and infinitely creative God.

In other words, CHaBaD denies nothing and embraces everything, seeing everything as the One Thing, God.

After the death of the Alter Rebbe in 1813, leadership of CHaBaD passed to his son, Dov Baer (1773–1827), and from Dov Baer to a succession of sons and sons-in-law. Over time, the movement set up its headquarters in Lubavitch (Lyubavichi, Russia), a town founded in the mid-seventeenth century and which grew to be a regional market center a century or so later. It is CHaBaD's historical link to Lubavitch that explains why CHaBaD Hasidim are also called Lubavitcher Hasidim, that is, the Hasidim from Lubavitch.

Over the five generations of rebbes following Schneur Zalman, CHaBaD Hasidism grew to be one of the largest Hasidic schools in Europe, establishing a growing network of religious, educational, and social institutions, which were designed to carry the teachings of CHaBaD throughout Europe.

In March 1940, the sixth Lubavitcher rebbe, Rabbi Joseph Isaac Schneersohn (1880–1950), escaped from Russia and certain death at the hands of the Nazis and made his way to the United States, where CHaBaD took root and flourished. With the passing of Rabbi Schneersohn, the leadership of the movement fell to his son-in-law, Rabbi Menachem M. Schneerson, who led his followers and expanded the movement worldwide until his death in 1994. Rabbi Schneerson did not designate a successor, and today CHaBaD is guided by the teachings of its historic rebbes, most especially by the wisdom of its last rebbe and the timeless wisdom of its first rebbe as articulated in *Tanya*.

Today CHaBaD Hasidism maintains more than thirty-three hundred communities in seventy-five countries, touching the lives of well over a million Jews. Many of these Jews, however, are not formally affiliated with CHaBaD but find in the teachings of the movement a school of Judaism that speaks to the heart and mind of many spiritual seekers. And this CHaBaD owes to the genius of its founder and the power of his central book of teaching, *Tanya*.

Key Philosophical Ideas ☐

Tanya presumes a level of kabbalistic knowledge that few of us have. I will do my best throughout this book to remind you of the meaning of the terms as they come up, and I have provided a glossary at the back of the book briefly defining the Hebrew terminology used by the Alter Rebbe, but it is wise and helpful to explore the following four ideas in some detail:

- *Shlemut*, the nonduality of God
- *YHVH* and *Ayn Sof*
- The five worlds/five intelligences
- *Kelipot* and *sitra achra*, distortions of reality

Each of these ideas could easily fill a book on its own. My concern here, however, is not to provide you with a historical overview of the origin and evolution of these ideas or to place them in their kabbalistic context. Rather, the goal of this section is to present these ideas in a manner that allows you to read and understand the selected *Tanya* translations presented in this book and to do so in a manner that enhances your own spiritual maturation.

God's Nonduality: *Shlemut*

Shlemut means "completeness" and refers to God's nonduality. *Shlemut* goes beyond the idea that God is One to an understanding that there is nothing other than God.

No doubt you have seen in some psychology book the black-and-white illustration used to explore the notion of figure and ground (see figure 1).

Figure 1

Looked at one way, the picture is a goblet. Looked at with a slight shift in focus, the goblet disappears to reveal the profiles of two people facing one another. Which is the true picture: the goblet or the faces?

The answer, of course, is both. What you see is called "figure"; what you don't see is called "ground." While your brain reacts to one or the other, you know intellectually that both figure and ground are present. Not only that, but figure and ground arise together; they are completely interdependent. The goblet is only visible because of the profiles, and the profiles are only visible because of the goblet. The interdependence and hence unity of figure and ground, however, is not yet *shlemut*, nonduality.

To grasp the idea of *shlemut* we must ask a different question. Not which is the more real, figure or ground, but what is the picture in and of itself? What is the picture when no one is looking at it?

Without a viewer, neither figure nor ground arises. Without a viewer, the graphic is neither goblet nor profiles. So what is it? It is something else, something we cannot define because to define it we must see it, and as soon as we look we no longer see it, but only the goblet or the profiles. The act of looking drives the "it" away. Or, to use language more akin to *Tanya*, the act of looking for "it" causes the "it" to hide. But it is hiding in plain sight. In other words, you are seeing it, but you have no way to recognize or articulate it. This is because our thinking and our language divide the world into objects we can compare and contrast, whereas the "it" has nothing outside itself to which it can be compared. In this sense, the "it" is God.

When you look for God's nonduality, you cannot see it, because the act of looking reveals duality rather than nonduality. And while it may be possible for you to know that all duality is part of a greater unity, the very notion of unity and diversity is dualistic and keeps nonduality hidden. Where is it hidden? Nowhere but in your own mind. You can't find it because your mind is incapable of seeing anything outside the range of the either/or choice of figure and ground.

YHVH and *Ayn Sof*

There is a greater reality that includes and transcends both figure and ground. This greater reality holds both figure and ground but is not limited by either. This is the reality *Tanya* calls *Ayn Sof* (literally: *Ayn*, "without"; *Sof*, "end"). *Ayn Sof* is God—but not God as something or somewhere, but God as all things and everywhere. *Ayn Sof* is the all of God that we call God's nonduality (*shlemut*). It is not simply that God is One, for one implies many. It is that God includes both the One and the many, both unity and diversity, both figure and ground in a greater reality.

Where is this reality? It is right in front of you. And behind, around, within, and beyond you as well. Why can't you see it? You do see it. In fact, you are it. But you cannot see it as separate from everything else. That is, you cannot make it a figure against a ground because it is not other than figure and ground.

Trying to see *Ayn Sof* as a figure is like trying to bite your own teeth or hear your own ear. You cannot make *Ayn Sof* an object of investigation because you are not other than it and cannot be separated from it. *Ayn Sof* is never an object, and when we speak of it as such, we are simply bumping up against the limits of language. *Ayn Sof* is the eternal subject, the "I" that is all things. This is what the prophet Isaiah is being told when God says, "I am *YHVH*, and there is none else" (Isaiah 45:5).

YHVH is most often translated into English as "Lord," implying that God is male, the head of a hierarchical quasi-military feudal structure, and far removed from the rest of us lowly serfs. While such an understanding no doubt serves the purposes of those religious leaders who benefit from hierarchical quasi-military feudal religious organizations, it has nothing to do with the Hebrew word *YHVH* at all.

While used as a proper Name of God in Torah, *YHVH* is in fact a verb, something akin to the future imperfect form of the Hebrew verb "to be." The meaning of the Name is explained in God's revelation to Moses at the Burning Bush. Moses inquires about God's Name, and God replies, *Ehyeh asher Ehyeh* (Exodus 3:14). Often mistranslated as "I am what I am," the Hebrew actually says, "I will be what I will be."

"I am" is static; "I will be" is dynamic. *YHVH* isn't a fixed name of an unchanging being, but an active, future-oriented verb hinting at an ever-moving, ever-creating, always-becoming creativity. At any given moment what is, is God. And, since God is never static or fixed, what is is never static or fixed. Everything is in flux. As the Jewish philosopher and interpreter of Hasidism Martin Buber put it:

> The world is a spinning die, and everything turns and changes: man is turned into angel, and angel into man, and the head into the foot, and the foot into the head. Thus all things turn and spin and change, this into that, and that into this, the topmost to the undermost, and the undermost to the topmost. For at the root all is one.[1]

Tanya reveals God as the *I* of the universe, the one true Self who is the multiplicity of selves you and I seem to encounter. All encounters are divine encounters: God meeting God on one level of reality or another. To see this, to know this, is to achieve *da'at devekut*, the realization that all things are united in, with, and as God.

Why do we see a multiplicity of I's? Indeed, why do we experience our own sense of "I" as separate from all other I's and from God as well? Because the "I," the egoic intelligence that gives rise to our sense of "I," "me," and "mine," is limited to seeing reality in terms of figure and ground. Change intelligences and a new dimension of reality is visible.

The Five Worlds/Five Intelligences

According to the Alter Rebbe, there are five intelligences we humans are capable of utilizing, and each intelligence reveals a dimension of reality that it alone can perceive. These five dimensions are called the five worlds.

The kabbalists speak of reality as a system of five concentric and interwoven worlds, or dimensions. Think of these as a set of Russian nesting dolls. Just as the smaller dolls are included in and transcended by the larger dolls, so the smaller worlds are included in and transcended by the larger. In Hebrew, the five worlds, beginning with the smallest or least inclusive, are *Assiyah, Yetzirah, Beriah, Atzilut,* and *Adam Kadmon.* The literal translations of these five dimensions are action, formation, creation, emanation, and primordial human, but from the human perspective they are better understood as physical, emotional, intellectual, social, and spiritual.

Think of these dimensions as frequencies of light. Just as the frequencies red, orange, yellow, green, blue, indigo, and violet are different frequencies within the spectrum of white light, so *Assiyah*, *Yetzirah*, *Beriah*, *Atzilut*, and *Adam Kadmon* are frequencies of the divine light, *Ayn Sof*.

Each of these dimensions has its own intelligence. This intelligence is the operating system of that dimension and provides the dimension with its unique way of knowing and perceiving reality. Again beginning with the least inclusive, the five intelligences are *Nefesh*, *Ruach*, *Neshamah*, *Chayyah*, and *Yechidah*, or body, heart, mind, soul, and spirit.

Nefesh is the innate wisdom of your body. It is how some cells know they are to be ears, while others know they are to be feet. *Nefesh* is how your autonomic nervous system knows how to be autonomic. *Nefesh* is impersonal and does not know you as a person. *Nefesh* functions whether you are a good person or a bad person. Indeed, *Nefesh* sometimes continues to function when you are no longer a person at all, as when the brain dies but the heart and lungs continue to function.

Ruach is the level of consciousness found in babies and young children. They encounter the world primarily through their feelings and instincts. For babies, life is quite simple: they feel pleasure or they feel pain. They gurgle with the former and cry with the latter. The entire function of *Ruach* can be summed up as grasping and avoiding. It grasps at what it likes, and seeks to avoid what it doesn't like. Simply put, *Ruach* is the intelligence of love and fear.

When a rock comes whizzing toward your head, you duck without thinking. That is *Ruach* in action. When your senses trigger deep feelings of joy, sadness, or fear without giving any warning that these emotions are about to dominate your awareness, that is *Ruach*. As you mature and actualize the higher levels of intellect, you can elevate *Ruach* beyond instinct and use it to generate deep and abiding love for one thing or, at its most elevated, all things. This most elevated state is called *Ruach HaKodesh*, the Holy Spirit that comes upon you when you experience deep awe and love. *Ruach HaKodesh* brings with it a deep emotional connection to all life and the Source of life. All of us have *Ruach* and the potential to develop it into *Ruach HaKodesh*, and *Tanya* speaks about how this can be accomplished.

Neshamah is self-reflective intelligence, the egoic operating system of the seemingly separate self. *Neshamah* is your capacity to say *I, me*, and *mine*. Where *Nefesh* is a body, *Neshamah* has a body. Where *Ruach* is feelings, *Neshamah* has feelings. *Neshamah* reveals the dimension of life called *Beriah*, where everything appears to be distinct and separate from everything else and from God. Indeed, *Neshamah's* conception of God is largely an extension of itself, seeing God as a supermind or superman.

Neshamah is absolutely essential to human life. As Rabbi Hillel (110 BCE–10 CE), one of the greatest of the early Rabbis, said, "If I am not for myself, who will be for me?" (*Pirke Avot* 1:14). A healthy person has a healthy ego, a strong sense of self-esteem, and a desire for self-improvement. And, as you mature, *Neshamah* realizes the truth of Hillel's balancing statement: "But if I am only for myself, then what am I?" If *Neshamah* is only for itself, it is selfish, isolated, lonely, and depressed. A mature *Neshamah* realizes that it must be for others as well as itself and that one of the best ways it can be for itself is to see to the welfare of others. The ethics of *Neshamah* is what we would call enlightened self-interest. You care for others because in the long run this is best for you.

The intelligence of *Neshamah* has access to three ways of knowing that, when combined, are called *seichel*, "intellect." Called the Three Mothers, these ways of knowing are *Chochmah, Binah*, and *Da'at*, or intuitive wisdom, rational understanding, and integrative knowledge. These are the tools *Neshamah* uses to overcome its limitations and open to the larger worlds and worldviews of *Atzilut* and *Adam Kadmon*, that is, the soul realm where all things are seen as parts of the singular reality we call God, and the nondual spirit realm where there are no things at all, just God.

When closed to these three ways of knowing, *Neshamah* sees itself as a separate self, alienated from and in competition with all other selves. It imagines and occupies a zero-sum world where the success of one necessitates the failure of others. This zero-sum worldview is called *sitra achra*, "the other side." *Sitra achra* is the other side of wholeness, abundance, and divine union, that is, the side of diversity, scarcity, and alienation from God.

The self *Neshamah* imagines itself to be is bounded, and that boundary is called the *kelipat nogah* ("a glittering shell"). While capable of illumination, the *kelipat nogah*, or separate self, appears as a solid boundary between self and other, and self and God. The boundary is illusory but seems real enough when viewed by *Neshamah* from the other side of wholeness (*sitra achra*).

When the *kelipat nogah* is illuminated, it is made transparent. This does not mean it disappears, but it no longer blocks the light coming to it from the more inclusive levels of consciousness, *Chayyah* (soul) and *Yechidah* (spirit). Think of *kelipat nogah* as a window covered by venetian blinds pulled closed. *Chayyah* is situated on one side of the window, and *Neshamah* (egoic self) on the other side, the *sitra achra*. On the unshaded *Chayyah* side, everything is seen to be what it is, a part of the singular reality of the Infinite Godhead (*Ayn Sof*). On the shaded *Neshamah* side, things appear in shadow and seem to have a separate existence of their own, independent of one another and of God.

No blind is solid enough to keep out all the light, and it is *Neshamah's* faculty of *Chochmah* that allows it to glimpse the enlightened world beyond the shade. *Chochmah*, wisdom, the first of the Three Mothers, is an intuitive insight into the suchness of reality as a finite expression of the Infinite Godhead (*Ayn Sof*). In *Tanya*, the Alter Rebbe plays with the word *chochmah*, suggesting that the true wisdom available to *Neshamah* is the capacity to see *choch*, the "suchness" or essential nature of *mah*, "what is."

Chochmah isn't a thought you think, but an insight you glimpse. It is something you suddenly, intuitively, know. You cannot say where the insight comes from, and as it is happening you cannot even say what it is you are grasping. It is a wordless glimpse beyond the venetian blind of *kelipat nogah* (separate self).

Chochmah intuits a brighter reality. When this intuition is triggered, it is passed on to *Binah*, rational understanding, the second of the Three Mothers. *Binah* is *Neshamah*'s faculty of reason. *Binah* takes the insight of *Chochmah* and begins to apply it to what it knows, challenging the status quo and improving its understanding of reality by incorporating the new insight into its worldview. *Binah* is the way you integrate new insights into your life.

Figuratively speaking, *Chochmah* and *Binah* are building a case for raising the blinds or at least enlarging the space between the slats to allow in more light.

Da'at, integrative knowledge, the third of the Three Mothers, literally means "knowing" and refers to your capacity to shape a worldview in accordance with intuition and reason that will lead to concrete action that sparks further intuitive glimpses into what is. Sticking with our metaphor, *Da'at* is the way you open the blinds.

How? By fashioning and living out of a worldview that, even in the shadow land of *Neshamah* (egoic self), honors the more illuminated worlds of *Atzilut/Chayyah* (soul) and *Adam Kadmon/Yechidah* (spirit). In other words, *Da'at* impels you to bring light into the shadowy world of *sitra achra* and to make clear the union of all things in, with, and as God. Or, to put it most simply, to open the blinds and bathe the darkened world of *Beriah* with the more intense light of *Atzilut*.

Atzilut is the social dimension where all things are seen to be interconnected. *Chayyah*, the intelligence of *Atzilut*, is transpersonal and is aware of the interconnectedness and interdependence of all life. *Chayyah* sees the self as no less unique than *Neshamah*, but no longer separate. To use Martin Buber's terminology, *Neshamah* sees the world from the perspective of I–It; there is me, and the rest of the world is a means to my ends. *Chayyah*, on the other hand, sees the world from the perspective of I–Thou: everything is of intrinsic value, and all things are expressions of the One Thing, God. We call *Chayyah* consciousness transpersonal because it lifts the *Neshamah* beyond itself. As you mature, *Chayyah* consciousness becomes almost totally transparent to the Divine. At the highest level of *Chayyah* consciousness, there is no thought of self or selfishness; all labels and loyalties are transcended, and you love each and all equally. This is the level achieved by our greatest saints.

If *Neshamah* is I–It, and *Chayyah* is I–Thou, the world of *Adam Kadmon* and the intelligence called *Yechidah* is I–I. We have stepped beyond Buber and are awake to the Infinite I that is all I's. From the perspective of *Yechidah*, all form is empty; there are no other worlds, selves, beings, or things—there is only God.

Yechidah is nonpersonal and absorbs the prior four dimensions into the nonduality of God. Here, thought, space, and time come to an end. It is toward *Yechidah* consciousness that Hillel points when he caps his teaching with "If not now, when?" From the perspective of *Yechidah*, now is the only time there is. Past and future are the projections of *Neshamah*. Indeed, past and future are the context in which *Neshamah* operates. When you step fully into the now, *Neshamah* is without a point of reference and simply drops away. Even *Chayyah* consciousness disappears as awareness of the nonduality of reality absorbs both the many and the One, the figure and the ground into the infinity of pure Godhead (*Ayn Sof*).

This self-emptying of *Yechidah*, however, is temporary, and is in no way the point of spiritual practice from *Tanya*'s perspective. On the contrary, the goal, if we can speak of goals, is to then return from *Yechidah* to *Neshamah* in order to engage the physical, emotional, and psychological dimensions of life in ways suffused with higher consciousness. That is to say, to hallow the ordinary—persons, places, and things—by engaging them justly and compassionately, seeing each thing as a manifestation of *Ayn Sof*. The goal of Jewish spirituality in general, and the Alter Rebbe's teachings in particular, is not to escape the lesser dimensions of reality for the greater, but to awaken the lesser to their participation in the greater, and in this way to unleash love for God and creation in all five dimensions.

The Other Side and the Separate Self: *Sitra Achra* and *Kelipat Nogah*

The Alter Rebbe understood the Ari's Kabbalah more as psychology than metaphysics. For him, the breaking of the vessels (*shevirat kelim*) was not an actual event happening in God, to God, but rather a metaphor for the way *Neshamah* perceives reality as a battle of separate selves competing for scarce resources. It is the isolated ego, as *Neshamah* might be called, that sees the world as broken, because it sees itself as alienated and alone.

Neshamah's perception of reality is limited to the less inclusive mental, emotional, and physical worlds (*Beriah*, *Yetzirah*, and *Assiyah*) because the light of the more inclusive worlds of *Atzilut* (the unitive world of soul) and *Adam Kadmon* (the nondual world of spirit) is blocked by *kelipat nogah*, the venetian blind of our earlier metaphor. This block gives *Neshamah* the false impression that there is a *sitra achra*, an other side to reality that is alienated from the whole and from God.

To understand *sitra achra*, imagine two people in a rowboat. After rowing far out into the center of a vast lake, one of the rowers sets down his oar and begins to drill a hole beneath his seat, letting water into the boat. His companion shouts for him to stop. "What are you doing?" she screams. "You are going to sink us both, and we will drown!"

"This is none of your concern," the man says as he continues to drill his hole. "This is my side of the boat, and I can do what I want. And what I want is to cool my feet with some water."

The ignorance of the man with the drill is a metaphor for the ignorance of *Neshamah* closed off to the light needed to reveal the fact that all living beings are in one boat, and that the acts of one impact the fate of all. This ignorance is the result of the darkness caused by the closed blinds. To end the ignorance, to correct the behavior, we must open the blinds.

The mechanism for opening the blinds is *Chochmah*, *Neshamah*'s capacity for intuitive wisdom, its ability to glimpse a world of light on the other side of the blind, and to inspire (with the help of *Binah* and *Da'at*, rational understanding and integrative knowledge) behaviors that will open the blinds and reveal a truer reality.

Opening the blinds and illuminating the shell of self is what *Tanya* is all about.

Core Spiritual Practices ☐

Throughout *Tanya* the Alter Rebbe emphasizes the importance of certain spiritual disciplines. His followers, of course, were all traditional Jews who were well versed in these practices. Chances are, however, you are not as well trained. The aim of this chapter is to present four of these disciplines in a manner that allows you to begin to practice them and does so with the hope that if you find them compelling, you will seek out further training on your own.

These four disciplines are Torah study, contemplative comprehension, breaking the heart, and *tzedakah*, which is acts of generosity and economic justice.

Torah Study

Throughout *Tanya* the Alter Rebbe makes reference to the study of Torah as a way of embodying God's will. The foundation of his claim is the teaching that God and Torah are one: when you study Torah you are delving into the very nature of God. Before we can take up the practice of Torah study, we had best find a way to understand the unity of Torah and God.

From the Alter Rebbe's perspective, Torah is the revealed word of God. As such, it represents the will of God in much the same way as a note from a parent instructing her or his child how and when to do certain chores represents the will of the parent who wrote it. For those followers of Torah who see the text in this way, carrying out the commandments (*mitzvot*) found in Torah is carrying out God's will. Hence, Torah and God are one, the former expressing the will of the latter. But not everyone reading this book will feel this way about Torah or God. I certainly don't.

For me, God is *Ayn Sof*, the infinite and infinitely creative *"Is-*ing" of the universe, and that greater unmanifest reality out of which the manifest cosmos emerges and into which it returns in a never-ending dance of *Yesh* and *Ayn*, "form" and "emptiness." God's will, as I understand it, is simply to be God. That is, God's will is to be true to God's nature that is the dance of creation, dissolution, and re-creation. God, as I understand God, does not write books or reveal them to individuals or to peoples. On the contrary, people write books, and all such books reflect the level of wisdom, as well as the conscious and unconscious biases and agendas, of the authors. Torah is no exception.

When the Alter Rebbe, citing the ancient Rabbis, reminds us that Torah is written in human language, he is most likely saying that God wants us to understand God's will and thus presents it to us in a manner we can understand, knowing that in so doing God is opening divine will to the limitations of human language. As humanity matures, deeper and deeper insights into Torah will result, further clarifying our understanding of God's will.

When I say that Torah is written in human language, I am saying that humans wrote it. Some of these authors were not interested in God or God's will, but only in their own power and prestige. But some of these authors were spiritual geniuses whose *Neshamah* was open to the more inclusive reality revealed by tapping into *Chayyah* and *Yechidah* levels of intelligence. In every generation there are people capable of seeing and living beyond the zero-sum game of egoic consciousness (*Neshamah*) and infusing the world of seeming separate and competing selves with love and compassion. They do this by achieving those more inclusive levels of consciousness that reveal the interdependence of all life in God (*Chayyah*) and ultimately the nonduality of all life as God (*Yechidah*). When I study Torah, I am looking to get past the material obsessed with power and control and delve into the material steeped in justice, love, and compassion.

One way to do this is to study Torah through the five worlds of body, heart, mind, soul, and spirit. Or, to be more accurate, through the first four of these five worlds, since the fifth world, *Adam Kadmon*, cannot be "worked" but only surrendered to. More on this below.

PaRDeS: An Entry to Paradise

My particular manner of Torah study is derived from the traditional model that Rabbi Schneur Zalman undoubtedly had in mind. This model has nothing to do with the academic parsing of ancient text and refers instead to the ancient rabbinic approach to Torah called *PaRDeS*.

Our sages taught that there are four levels to any given passage of Torah: *peshat*, the simple or literal reading; *remez*, the allegorical reading; *drash*, the interpretive reading; and *sod*, the mystical reading. Together these are referred to by the acronym *PaRDeS*, which is the Hebrew word for "orchard," referring to the Garden of Eden and paradise. If you can hold all four levels together in your mind at the same time, you will enter paradise.

Such a claim needs some explanation. First of all, what does it mean to hold these four dimensions of Torah simultaneously? Second, what is paradise? And, third, how does the first lead to the second?

The four levels of reading do not fit neatly into a whole. *Peshat* need not lead to *remez*; nor does *remez* necessarily lead to *drash*, and *drash* doesn't inevitably lead to *sod*. Each reading is complete in and of itself and may well be antithetical to one or more of the others.

Take the story of Noah and the Flood, for example. On the *peshat*/literal level, we are talking about a literal drowning of all beings with the exception of those that are ushered into Noah's ark. On the *remez*/allegorical level, we note that the name *Noah* means "equanimity" and that the story can be read as a parable of how one maintains equanimity in times of calamity. On the *drash*/interpretive level, there is the fact that the word for ark, *teva*, can be connected to the word *tavot*, "letters," and thus we have a homily about taking refuge in the words of Torah in times of crisis. On the *sod*/mystical level, we note that the ark is equipped with a skylight, suggesting that taking refuge in words, no matter how sacred, can be a trap unless there is space (the window) through which fresh air and light (divine spirit and wisdom) can come in. Learning how to make space for the spirit is the challenge of the Noah story in this reading.

Each reading is interesting and valuable in and of itself, irrespective of the other three. And they do not fit neatly into some meta-reading. Either the ark is a boat or it is sacred text, but it cannot be both. Or can it?

On the logical level the answer is no, it cannot. Logic demands that a thing is either itself or not itself; "A" is "A" only and never "Not A." But logic is not the end-all of human thinking. Human beings, perhaps alone among the species of the earth, can hold paradox. We can open our minds wide enough to include the statements "A is A" and "A is Not A" at the very same time. It is paradox that keeps things fresh, multidimensional, fluid. It is paradox and the ability to be comfortable with paradox that is at the heart of *PaRDeS*.

The answer to our first question, "What does it mean to hold these four dimensions of Torah simultaneously?" is this: it means to be comfortable with paradox. It means to have a mind spacious enough to hold both "A" and "Not A" and not feel compelled to choose one over the other.

The answer to our second question, "What is paradise?" flows directly from the answer to the first. Paradise is the ability to hold paradox. Paradise, nirvana, enlightenment, spiritual awakening (I use all four terms interchangeably) is *mochin d'gadlut*, "spacious mind," a mind capable of holding paradox.

Working with the multidimensional Torah forces the narrow mind (*mochin d'katnut*) beyond narrowness and either/or thinking to spaciousness or enlightened thinking. *Mochin d'gadlut* is a mind without boundaries, a mind capable of engaging infinite possibility, a mind that allows for all things and yet identifies with no thing. It is the ocean upon which and in which the waves of thoughts and feelings rise and fall of their own accord.

The answer to our third question—"How does working with the *PaRDeS* model of Torah lead to *PaRDeS* mind?"—is, it doesn't. It is

PaRDeS mind. To operate in *PaRDeS* is to be in *mochin d'gadlut*, spacious mind.

It is important to grasp the implications of this for the study of Torah. Torah study is not a way to anything. It is the way of the thing itself. This is what is meant by the term *Torah lishmah*, studying Torah for Her own sake.

The Alter Rebbe, again resting on ancient rabbinic teaching, reminds us that the highest level of Torah study is *Torah lishmah*. We do not study to earn fame or merit, or even to learn something; we study simply to study. In other words, we study Torah because the spacious mind needed for the study of Torah is the mind open to *PaRDeS*, enlightenment, the realization that all things are facets of the One Thing, God.

According to the first-century-CE sage Ben Bag Bag, we generate spacious mind by turning Torah: "Turn Her and turn Her for all things are in Her" (*Pirke Avot* 5:22). The "Her" is Torah, but not simply the scroll itself, but the wisdom that the scroll embodies. Torah is not an inanimate being but the living wisdom of God glimpsed by spiritual geniuses in the past and articulated in the language of their time to trigger our own awakening in our own time.

When we take a word or phrase of Torah and begin to work with it, the work we do is called turning. Turning means that we use the text to trigger one insight after another in our minds. The more we turn, the more possibilities we see. We never stop at one or two. We do not allow our minds to attach to any insight but continue to turn and turn the text until the flow of wisdom overwhelms the simple linear thinking of the egoic, narrow, *Neshamah* mind. In other words, we slip from *mochin d'katnut*, the narrow mind associated with *Neshamah* consciousness, to *mochin d'gadlut*, the spacious mind associated with *Chayyah* consciousness. And, in those rare moments when we are completely lost in the turning, we are surrendered to *Yechidah* consciousness and "experience" *bittul*, self-emptying; we slip into the nondual awareness of *Yechidah* consciousness that sees both the narrow and the spacious, all worlds and all awareness, as the infinite play of God. At that moment the turning is no longer work, but sheer delight. Torah study becomes Torah play, true *lishmah*. You are home, *PaRDeS*, paradise.

CONNECTING *PaRDeS* WITH FOUR WORLDS: A PRACTICE
Thus far we are still within the parameters of traditional Torah turning. Now I want to add something of my own, linking the four types of turning to the first four of the five worlds and then offering a way of tapping the intelligence associated with each world through a particular type of turning.

The first or literal level of turning, *peshat*, is linked to the least inclusive of the five worlds, *Assiyah*, and its corresponding consciousness, *Nefesh*, the intelligence of the body. When turning Torah, begin with the *Assiyah* level.

Read aloud the text you are turning (or, even better, have a study partner read it to you). As you listen to the text, become aware of *Nefesh*, the intelligence of the body. How is your body reacting to what is being heard? Does the text cause the body to constrict or expand? Is there discomfort anywhere in your body as the text is read? Does it speak to one part of the body or another? Why does this text cause your body to react this way? What is Torah saying to you through *Nefesh* consciousness? If you are turning alone, write your answers in a journal. If you are turning with a partner, share the insights of *Nefesh* aloud as well.

When you have explored the text from the level of *peshat* and noted the body's response to Torah, move on to the second level, *remez*. *Remez* is associated with the world of *Yetzirah* and *Ruach*, the intelligence of the heart. Listen to the text a second time, and turn your attention to your heart. What emotions are triggered by Torah? Does Torah generate feelings of love or fear, gratefulness or shame, tranquility or anger? Ask yourself why these feelings might be triggered with this turning of Torah? Share these as well, either in your journal or with your partner, or both.

When you have honored the heart's response to Torah through *remez*, move on to *drash*. *Drash* is linked to the world of *Beriah*, mind, and the egoic intelligence of *Neshamah*. Listen to the text a third time, and turn your attention to the egoic mind. What ideas are triggered by Torah? What memories from your own life, the lives of others, or the life of your people or community, long past or sharply present, does this reading evoke? How does this passage of Torah challenge or confirm your ideas about yourself, life, and how best to live it? What, if anything, troubles you about this reading? Share these insights with your partner, and/or note them in your journal.

When you have exhausted the ego's response to Torah (at least for now), move on to the fourth level of turning, *sod*. *Sod* is associated with the world of *Atzilut* and its operating intelligence, *Chayyah*, transpersonal soul. Listen to Torah a fourth time, and pay attention to *Chayyah*, the intelligence that sees all life as interdependent, all lives as part of a single living system itself a manifestation of the One Life, God. Here you imagine that you are the characters about which you are reading, as well as the place in which the drama unfolds. Everything you read is a reflection of your life. Torah is a mirror reflecting your life. Allow your imagination to have free play here and see what arises. How is *Chayyah* turning you as you are turning Torah?

There is no fifth turning. There is no method for actualizing the world of *Adam Kadmon* and the nondual level of consciousness called *Yechidah*, for this level of knowing is not grasped but received. When the other four turnings are operating, there is a loosening of narrow mind and a slipping into spacious mind. If this continues long enough, spacious mind becomes pure spaciousness, what the Alter Rebbe calls *gadlut Elohit*, "the unending spaciousness of God." Here your entire being is surrendered, and there is no "I" other than the "I" of God. All sense of you is gone; all sense of other is gone. There is only God.

Contemplative Comprehension: *Tevunah*

Torah turning is one way you can invite *bittul*, the emptying of self into the infinite spaciousness of God. Not everyone, however, has the capacity to turn Torah to the point of *lishmah*, pure play and self-emptying. Awakening to the Presence of God in and as all reality is not limited to Torah turners alone. There are other ways to God realization explored in *Tanya*, among them the practice of *tevunah*, contemplative comprehension of God's infinite and all-encompassing nature.

I teach *tevunah* using two Hebrew texts. The first is from the daily Jewish liturgy, *Esa einai el heharim, me'ayin yavo ezri*, "I lift up my eyes to the mountains; from whence [*me'ayin*] will my help come?" (Psalm 121:1). The mystical meaning of the prayer comes from the play on the words *Ayn* and *ayin*. Read mystically as *me'ayn* rather than *me'ayin*, the text says, "I lift up my eyes to the mountains; from the Divine No–thing [God] my help comes."

The second text is *Shiviti Adonai l'negdi tamid* (Psalm 16:8). While the literal meaning of the Hebrew is "I place God before me always," the mystical understanding is "I see God equally before me always." That is, whatever I see is a manifestation of God.

The practice is this: Sit comfortably outdoors or in front of a window that allows you a view of the outdoors, and lift your eyes gently so that they rest on the horizon. If you have hills or mountains to provide you with a focal point, rest your gaze on the point at which they meet the sky. If not, gently lift your eyes skyward so that you see nothing in particular and simply gaze at the vastness of the sky. Begin by reciting or chanting, *Esa einai el heharim, me'ayin yavo ezri*. Do this simply to settle the mind, and when you feel settled, cease the repetition. Do not control your thoughts or even take excessive note of them. Whatever arises in your mind, let it go. Do not become angry with yourself if thoughts and feelings continue to arise; these are not under your control. Rather, greet each one as another opportunity to surrender; that is, let it rise and fall of its own accord without your active participation at all. If your mind becomes agitated, return to *Esa einai*, but do not make it a rote repetition. Let it go when the mind is once again calm. In time, a sense of growing spaciousness will arise in you. Your mind will become as wide as the sky, making room for whatever clouds arise without identifying with any of them.

Practice this for twenty to thirty minutes, and then shift your gaze to the world around you. See everything from the perspective of emptiness (*Ayn*) and spacious mind (*mochin d'gadlut*), and remind yourself, *Shiviti Adonai l'negdi tamid*—everything you see is a form of the formless, a manifestation of God. If you practice this several times each week, you will find that you spend more and more of your day in this state of spacious awareness, engaging form (*Yesh*) with an openness arising from emptiness (*Ayn*), and knowing both to be aspects of God.

Breaking the Heart

Not everyone finds Torah study and *PaRDeS* doable. To these people, as well as to those who want to add another practice to their spiritual lives, the Alter Rebbe offers a third: the practice of breaking the heart.

Just as a log is more easily burned when splintered, so the heart is more easily aroused to love when broken. Breaking the heart cultivates humility by focusing your attention on the suffering you cause yourself and others when you engage the world selfishly.

The practice is simple: Pay attention to the damage you do through your thoughts, words, and deeds. These are called the Three Garments and represent the three ways in which your intellect manifests itself in the world. Because the *Neshamah* level of intelligence imagines it occupies a zero-sum reality where your success often requires another's failure, living from *Neshamah* consciousness exclusively (i.e., to the exclusion of *Chayyah* and *Yechidah* consciousness) means living with a sense of anxiety so strong as to make both happiness and compassion almost impossible for you to achieve. You are always looking over your shoulder to see who is about to pass you on the race to success and always looking for an advantage to bring down the person in front of you in the same race.

All you want to achieve is a level of happiness; all you manage to achieve is an ever-increasing level of suffering. Becoming aware of this suffering is the key to ending it.

You splinter the self by constantly admitting to the suffering it is causing both itself and others. The task here is simply to pay attention to the body (*Nefesh*) and heart (*Ruach*) levels of consciousness.

For example, when a choice you make causes your body to constrict, to take a defensive posture, to recoil, it may be that *Nefesh* is telling you that what you are doing is not right. Similarly, if *Ruach* feels fearful, anxious, or angry, your heart may be telling you that this is not the right course to follow. Pay attention to *Nefesh* and *Ruach*, the intelligences of your body and heart, but not only yours.

As you engage with others during the day, pay attention to their *Nefesh* and *Ruach* reactions to your presence. Are they hunkering down, showing signs of fear and anguish? These are clear signs that what you are doing is causing suffering.

At first the *Neshamah*'s insistence on zero-sum thinking will excuse the suffering of others as a necessary and unavoidable consequence of pursuing your own happiness. But as you look more closely, as the pain you cause becomes more apparent to you, it robs you of your happiness. You begin to realize that there is no private happiness at the expense of another. You begin to suspect that there is more to you than you.

By observing the suffering you cause, *Neshamah*'s capacity to intuit the wisdom of *Chayyah* consciousness, to glimpse the greater truth of the interdependence of yourself and others, is aroused, and *Neshamah* begins to question the rightness of its actions and the worldview that supports them. As the questioning deepens, *Neshamah* opens to *Chayyah*, and you no longer feel apart from others but a part of them.

With this new awareness, selfishness is no longer excusable, and your heart breaks under the burden of all the selfish and hurtful acts you have committed. *Neshamah* is splintered, and the more inclusive awareness of *Chayyah* becomes the norm. Everything changes and you begin to act in accordance with Hillel's teaching, "If I am not for myself, who will be for me; but if I am only for myself, of what value am I?" *If I am not for myself, who will be for me*—there is a place for *Neshamah* consciousness; but *if I am only for myself, of what value am I?*—only as long as it is subservient to *Chayyah* consciousness. This is the knowing that shapes all future action, balancing the needs of the one with the needs of the many, seeing them all as part of the One.

Tzedakah

Tzedakah is the just earning and use of finances in service to both self and others. The Alter Rebbe calls *tzedakah mitzvah stam*, the foundational spiritual practice. He says this because he believes that it can be done by anyone. In *Tanya*, *tzedakah* is primarily used in the context of giving money to the poor. In the Alter Rebbe's day, *tzedakah* was a central obligation of Jewish life, regardless of a person's economic station or spiritual accomplishments.

> Life in the shtetl begins and ends with tzedakah. When a child is born, the father pledges a certain amount of money for distribution to the poor. At a funeral the mourners distribute coins to the beggars who swarm the cemetery, repeating, "Tzedakah saves from death."
>
> At every turn during one's life, the reminder to give is present…. Every celebration, every holiday, is accompanied by gifts to the needy. Each house has its round tin box into which coins are dropped for the support of various good works. A home that is not very poor will have a series of such boxes, one for the synagogue, one for a yeshiva in some distant city, one for "clothing the naked," one for "tending the sick," and so on. If something good or bad happens, one puts a coin into the box. Before lighting the Sabbath candles, the housewife drops a coin into one of the boxes….
>
> Children are trained in the habit of giving. A father will have his son give alms to the beggar instead of handing them over directly. A child is very often put in charge of the weekly dole at home, when beggars make their customary rounds. The gesture of giving becomes almost a reflex.[1]

While there are many traditions surrounding the giving of *tzedakah,* the reason it plays such a powerful role in *Tanya* is its capacity to remind you that the other is not other at all, but part of the One. The commandment to "love your neighbor as yourself" (Leviticus 19:18) is not a command to feel as loving toward another as you do toward yourself, but to love your neighbor as part of your self; that is, to realize that the other is a part of you and you are a part of the other and both are manifestations of God. Indeed, giving *tzedakah* leads to the realization that there is no self or other and that giving to the needy is like taking money from your right hand and placing it into your left.

The reason *tzedakah* is a practice in which anyone can engage is hinted at by the word itself. Unlike the word "charity," which has its origins in the Latin *caritas*, "heart," *tzedakah* comes from the Hebrew word *tzedek*, "justice." Charity requires an awakening of heart intelligence (*Ruach*), something not everyone can accomplish. *Tzedakah*, on the other hand, challenges you to be just, a virtue that the scarcity-fearing egoic consciousness (*Neshamah*) is quite willing to support, since creating a system of just earning and use of finances protects you as well as others.

Moses Maimonides, the great medieval physician and philosopher, set forth eight degrees of *tzedakah* (with number 1 being the ultimate and number 8 being the most basic) still followed today:

1. Seeing to a person's independence by providing a person with a job, entering into a partnership that allows the person to establish a business, giving an interest-free loan, giving a grant.
2. Giving *tzedakah* anonymously through a reputable third party and without knowing who will receive the aid.
3. Giving anonymously to a known recipient.
4. Giving publically to an unknown recipient.
5. Giving without being asked.
6. Giving generously after being asked.
7. Giving gladly but not generously.
8. Giving grudgingly.[2]

Tanya doesn't speak to how *tzedakah* is to be practiced, because the Alter Rebbe assumed his readers would know. And for our purposes, going into the details of Jewish *tzedakah* practice would take us too far afield. What we need here is a simple way to practice *tzedakah* that draws from Judaism without necessarily imitating it.

Keeping the practice as simple as possible, I suggest the following: First, do your best to see that the money you earn is earned in a manner that does as little harm to the environment and other people as possible. Knowing that each person's situation is unique, I won't presume to set fixed guidelines here and only ask you to take a hard look at your work and its impact on the world.

Assuming your money is earned ethically and morally, and with as little damage to nature as possible, and assuming that you will regularly do what you can to improve on this as opportunities for economic and environmental justice present themselves, you should set aside a fixed amount (Judaism says 10 percent) of your income to distribute to the poor.

You can do this by donating the money to a fund run by others, setting up an interest-free loan society in your own community, giving money out of your wallet or purse when asked, or any other system or combination of systems you see fit. The key is to use that 10 percent for *tzedakah* and nothing else.

Tanya speaks of *tzedakah* in the context of one-to-one giving, and it may be in that context that its capacity for spiritual awakening is most powerful. While it is right and good to contribute to the welfare of others through formal giving to organizations devoted to such work, it does keep you from confronting the needy directly. It is the direct engagement with people in need that makes spiritual awakening through *tzedakah* possible.

When you sincerely engage with a person in need, even though you do so out of a sense of justice and obligation rather than heartfelt charity, your heart, *Ruach*, cannot help but be moved. Unlike charity, you need not be moved before you give—*tzedakah* is an obligation, not an emotional choice—but you will be moved by the act of giving. Feelings follow behavior in the practice of *tzedakah*, rather than precede behavior as in the practice of charity.

When the heart is aroused, you discover, as the Alter Rebbe says, that you are the vehicle for God's justice. More and more you begin to perceive the unjust nature and randomness of the circumstances into which people are born and are aroused to do something to move the system toward justice.

Moreover, as you help others with your gifts of generosity, you begin to notice and appreciate the gifts that you have received as well. You realize that you are who you are because of those who have gifted you along the way: supportive parents, good teachers, friends sharing your values and supporting your dreams, business mentors who showed you the ropes and helped you climb them. You realize that you are a product of all the gifts you have been given.

With this realization comes another, the key one, since all you have and are is in some sense a gift—it doesn't really belong to you. It was gifted to you that you might gift it to another. Since all things are manifestations of God, you are simply part of the divine system of justice that shares the wealth of one to meet the needs of another. This removes any hubris from the act of *tzedakah* and humbles the *Neshamah*, opening it to the realization that self and other are each part of the greater oneness that is God and, perhaps, even to the knowledge that self and other are God.

Tanya,
the Masterpiece
of Hasidic Wisdom

[1] Talmud, *Niddah* 30b.

[2] *Pirke Avot* 2:13.

[3] Gemara is the later part of the Talmud, written between 250 and 550 CE.

[4] Talmud, *Berachot* 7a provides the first four categories; *Rosh Hashanah* 16b provides the fifth.

[5] *Beinoni*, literally "an inbetweener," is a person who is neither saint nor sinner, but one who has elements of both.

[6] *Yetzer hatov*, "the good inclination," the inclination toward selfless service to others.

[7] *Yetzer hara*, "the evil inclination," the inclination toward selfishness.

1 □ The Five Kinds of Humans

Our Sages taught,
Before you were born you were taught,
and before you were born you promised:
"Be righteous and not wicked,
and even if the entire world calls you righteous,
consider yourself wicked."[1]
This teaching seems to contradict an older one,
"Do not regard yourself as wicked."[2]

The Gemara[3] resolves this contradiction,
teaching us that humans can be divided into five categories:[4]
the righteous who succeed in erasing all selfishness,
the righteous who fail to erase all selfishness,
the wicked who succeed in holding on to some inkling of
        selflessness,
the wicked who fail to consider anything or anyone but
        themselves,
and the inbetweener.[5]

The righteous who succeed
are those who are motivated solely by their inclination toward
        selflessness.[6]
The righteous who fail
are those who wrestle with yet control their inclination toward
        selfishness[7]

(continued on page 5)

3

8 | Kehot edition, p. 1.

≋ | The *beinoni*, literally "the inbetweener," is someone with the capacity for both good and evil, who continually struggles to "turn from evil and do good" (Psalm 34:15). "Turning from evil" means expanding your consciousness from *Neshamah*, the egoic intelligence that sees the *Beriah* world of independent and competing selves, to *Chayyah*, the soul intelligence that sees reality as *Atzilut*, a world of interdependent and cooperating selves. "Doing good" is acting for the welfare of both self and other rooted in the understanding of the unity of self and other.

Neshamah and *Chayyah* are two of the five intelligences to which you have access. Each intelligence sees reality in its own way. In addition to *Neshamah* and *Chayyah*, there are *Nefesh*, the intelligence of the world of *Assiyah*, preconscious matter; *Ruach*, the intelligence of the world of *Yetzirah*, instinctual drives and feelings; and *Yechidah*, the intelligence of the world of *Adam Kadmon*, where all things are seen as the One Thing, God.

All five intelligences are operating all the time. The world you perceive depends on the intelligence you use to see it. Where the righteous strive to escape the "lower" worlds of *Assiyah*, *Yetzirah*, and *Beriah* for the higher worlds of *Atzilut* and *Adam Kadmon*, and the wicked deny there are any higher worlds at all, the *beinoni* seeks to understand the system as a whole and hallow all worlds through acts of love.

The wicked who succeed
are those who wrestle with but fail to control their inclination
toward selfishness.[8]
The wicked who fail
are those who are motivated solely by their inclination toward
selfishness.
The inbetweener is motivated by both inclinations
and must continually struggle to bind the selfish to the selfless.

1 Job 31:2.

2 Genesis 2:7.

3 *Penimiyut,* "inwardness." God blew life into you from the innermost depths of divinity.

4 *Chochmah.*

5 Maimonides, *Mishneh Torah, Hilchot Yesodei HaTorah* 2:10.

6 Job 11:7.

7 Isaiah 55:8.

2 □ God, Wisdom, and Your Essential Nature

The inclination toward selflessness is "a part of God above"[1]
as it is written,
"And He blew into his nostrils the breath of life."[2]

Blowing comes from the innermost depths of your being,[3]
so your very life, your innermost essence,
is the innermost essence of God.

This innermost essence manifests in you
as divine wisdom.[4]
But the wisdom of God is not knowable
the way other wisdom is knowable, for
"God is simultaneously Knower, Knowledge, and Known."[5]

This is what you are told when you read,
"Can you find God by searching?"[6]
and what God reveals to you saying,
"My thoughts are not your thoughts."[7]
God and wisdom are one,
and God being unknowable
makes wisdom unknowable as well.

(continued on page 9)

8 Psalm 104:24.

9 Kehot edition, p. 5.

≣ What is your true nature, your *penimiyut?* Each of the five intelligences answers from its own perspective. For *Nefesh* it is matter, for *Ruach* it is biological drives, for *Neshamah* it is will and power, for *Chayyah* it is love, and for *Yechidah* it is wisdom. While none is false, *Yechidah* is the most true, for nonduality perceived by *Yechidah* sees all five as variations of God. This is what wisdom is: the realization that all is God.

This wisdom is already within you (Psalm 104:24), indeed it is you, and you can no more seek it out than you can bite your own teeth. What you need to do is cease to be distracted by the glittering shell of self and selfishness (*kelipat nogah*) and see reality as it is: the infinite outpouring of the infinite God.

As the Alter Rebbe will explain, you do this by placing yourself in situations of overwhelming love, awe, and humility and in this way awaken the facility of *Chochmah,* wisdom, which makes transparent the otherwise opaque shell of self, allowing *Neshamah* to be surrendered to *Chayyah,* the way the light of a single burning candle is surrendered in the noonday sun.

And yet all beings have their essence
and root in the divine wisdom,
as it is written,
"You have made them all with wisdom."[8, 9]

1 *Nefesh*, *Ruach*, and *Neshamah*, the physical, emotional, and egoic intelligences, respectively.

2 The ten *sefirot* (literally "numbers") are the building blocks of creation.

3 *Chochmah*, *Binah*, and *Da'at*.

4 *Chesed*, *Gevurah*, *Tiferet*, *Netzach*, *Hod*, *Yesod*, and *Malchut*. Each day of the week has it own quality (*middah*), beginning with Sunday/*Chesed*/compassion.

5 *Seichel*.

6 *Middot*.

7 This is a pun on the word *chochmah*. Splitting the word in two, the Alter Rebbe understands wisdom as the capacity to intuit the suchness (*choch*) of what is (*mah*).

≣ The inbetweener doesn't reject, transcend, or escape body, heart, or egoic mind (*Nefesh*, *Ruach*, *Neshamah*), for they, no less than soul and spirit (*Chayyah* and *Yechidah*), are manifestations of God. On the contrary, the inbetweener activates the innate wisdom, understanding, and knowing (the Three Mothers) that reside in body, heart, and mind and cultivates their respective capacities for compassion, justice, balance, persistence, surrender, direction, and groundedness (the Seven Days).

8 Kehot edition, pp. 9–11.

3 □ The Three Mothers: Wisdom, Reason, and Knowing

The intelligences of body, heart, and egoic mind[1]
manifest through the ten emanations.[2]

These emanations are divided into two categories:
The Three Mothers—Intuitive Wisdom, Rational
     Understanding, and Integrative Knowledge[3] and
The Seven Days—Compassion, Justice, Balance, Persistence,
     Surrender, Direction, and Groundedness.[4]

The Three Mothers are intellect, the quality of discernment.[5]
The Seven Days are the qualities of godliness you are to
     cultivate.[6]
The Three Mothers are called mothers
because they give birth to the seven qualities of godliness.

Intuitive wisdom is first among the Mothers,
intuiting the essence of what is.[7]
Rational understanding filters intuition through reason,
birthing integrative knowledge, the knowledge of things as
     they are.
Together the Mothers reveal the qualities of godliness.[8]

1 The *Neshamah* (egoic self) impacts the world primarily through thought, word, and deed. When your *Neshamah* is aware of its place in the divine whole, your thoughts, words, and deeds serve the welfare of the whole. When such awareness is lacking, they serve only yourself.

2 When you live justly, kindly, and humbly (Micah 6:8).

3 When your words heal rather than harm.

4 When your thoughts dwell on the nonduality of God.

5 The 613 *mitzvot*, or sacred commandments and spiritual practices, contained in the Torah are divided into two categories: 248 positive or prescribed actions and 365 negative or prohibited ones. Simply put, the positive *mitzvot* are actions that hallow life, while negative *mitzvot* prohibit actions that denigrate it.

6 Kehot edition, p. 15.

7 Psalm 145:3.

8 Talmud, *Megillah* 31a.

9 Kehot edition, p. 15.

4 □ The Three Garments: Thought, Word, and Deed

The degree to which the egoic intelligence
is awake to its divine core
is revealed through Three Garments:
thought, speech, and action.[1]
When you live Torah,[2]
speak Torah,[3]
and think Torah[4]
you are fully alive.

Living Torah is love,
for the positive practices[5] are grounded in love,
and living them is loving God,
for God and Torah are one.[6]

The vastness of God "can never be plumbed,"[7]
Yet godliness is known.
Godliness is humility,
as it is written,
"Where you find the vastness of God,
you find God's humility."[8, 9]

(continued on page 15)

10 Kehot edition, p. 17.

≣ Torah (literally "instruction") manifests in five dimensions corresponding to the five worlds. The Torah of *Assiyah* is "Do I not fill heaven and earth?" (Jeremiah 23:24); the Torah of *Yetzirah* is "You shall love your neighbor as yourself" (Leviticus 19:18); the Torah of *Beriah* is "Justice, justice you shall pursue" (Deuteronomy 16:20); the Torah of *Atzilut* is "You shall love the Infinite your God with fullness of heart, with spaciousness of soul, and with all you have and are" (Deuteronomy 6:5); and the Torah of *Adam Kadmon* is "I am the One and Only, there is nothing other than Me" (Isaiah 45:5). When you live Torah in each dimension, the thoughts, words, and deeds you bring into the world are expressions of wisdom.

The way of the inbetweener is the way of Torah, doing *mitzvot* to realize the unity of all worlds in the singular reality of God.

This is why Torah is compared to water.
Just as water flows from the highest to the lowest,
so Torah, the wisdom of God,
flows from the most transcendent
to the most immanent,
so that every life is bound up in Life.[10]

[1] *Tikkunei Zohar*, Introduction, 17a.

[2] Hence no thought can grasp God, but God can grasp the thinker.

[3] Kehot edition, p. 17.

[4] Intellect (*seichel*) is composed of *Chochmah*, *Binah*, and *Da'at* (intuitive wisdom, rational understanding, and integrative knowledge). When these three faculties of the mind are open to one another and to the more inclusive intelligence of *Chayyah*, you realize all is God.

5 □ Unity Beyond Thought

How shall we understand the words of Elijah,
"No thought can grasp You?"[1]

When you think a thought,
you are greater than that thought.
But when that thought is of Torah,
which is rooted in God,
the thought is greater than you,
and you become absorbed into the thought,
and in this way you and God are one.[2, 3]

This is a glorious union unlike any other.
It has no parallel in the material world,
for the unity is complete
from every side and every perspective,
something that occurs only
when the mind is invested in Torah
and at one with God.

Hence the command to know Torah,
rather than to merely study Torah,
is in fact a command to know God
by allowing your intellect to be suffused
with the divine light that is Torah.[4]

(continued on page 19)

5 Psalm 40:9.

6 *Torah lishmah,* studying Torah "for its own sake," which is to achieve union with God.

7 Kehot edition, p. 21.

☰ God is beyond thought, but Torah is not. You cannot grasp God, but you can grasp godliness. When you engage Torah study for its own sake (*Torah lishmah*), selflessly and for the sole purpose of embodying godliness, your mind becomes absorbed in Torah. And, because Torah is the expression of God as godliness, your mind is absorbed in God.

Imagine a fresh sponge submerged in a tub of water. The longer it stays submerged, the more the water fills every facet of its being. In time, the sponge and the water are one. *Neshamah* is like this sponge. The longer your intellect (*seichel*) is engaged with Torah, the more it realizes that it is filled with God. In time, it comes to the realization of *da'at devekut*, the knowledge of the absolute unity of all things in, with, and as God.

This is not the highest union, for there is still a knower; the *Neshamah* is not lost to itself, just no longer lost in itself. Yet this level of realization shatters the *Neshamah's* false sense of alienation and leaves *Neshamah* motivated to live Torah by doing justly, loving mercy, and walking humbly (Micah 6:8).

This is the meaning of the teaching,
"Yea, Your Torah is within my inward parts,"[5]
which is to say that God's wisdom permeates all life.
And this is what is meant by
engaging with Torah with the sole intent
of achieving union with God[6]
by concentrating your mind to the best of your ability.[7]

1 Ecclesiastes 7:14.

2 Thought, word, and deed.

3 *Sitra achra* ("other side"), your sense of being cut off from God.

4 *Kelipat nogah* ("glittering shell"), your sense of separate selfhood. It is called *nogah*, "glittering," because it distracts the *Neshamah* from the greater truth of its unity with God.

5 Just as front goes with back, so the One goes with the many. God is not limited to either, but manifests and transcends them both.

6 Kehot edition, pp. 21–23.

≣ The nonduality of God (*shlemut*) necessitates the manifestation of all things and their opposite. The *sitra achra* is the other side of God's oneness, the side that insists that it is other than and alienated from God. Why would God choose to manifest in this way? It is not a matter of choice. God has no choice but to be God, and being God means manifesting everything and its opposite. Just as a magnet doesn't choose to have a negative pole, so God doesn't choose to manifest *sitra achra*. Just as a magnet cannot be a magnet without both positive and negative poles, so God cannot be God without both sides. The *sitra achra*, while being the source of self, selfishness, and evil, is not, in and of itself, evil. It is, as all things are, part of the infinite creativity of God. The task of the inbetweener is not to eliminate *sitra achra*, but to enlighten it.

6 □ The Necessity of Opposites

Everything has its opposite, as it is written,
"God has created one thing and the other."[1]

Just as the Three Garments[2]
when rooted in godliness
reflect selflessness,
so when rooted in the other side[3]
they reflect your sense of being a separate self.[4]

The Garments absorbed in God are godly.
The Garments absorbed in self are petty.

Yet even the other side is necessary,
veiling the pure light of God
to create the illusion of other
that the other might yet come to know the One.[5, 6]

1 Because everything is part of God, everything can be used in the service of godliness.

2 Talmud, *Yoma* 76b. The Talmudic sage Rava claimed that drinking wine made him more receptive to discovering the inner meanings of Torah.

3 Maimonides, *Mishneh Torah, Hilchot Shabbat* 30:7; *Hilchot Yom Tov* 6:16.

7 □ Using the Body for Good

Physical desire is necessarily selfish,
seeing the body as an end in itself,
rather than a means of divine service.

Yet even physical desire
contains a spark of holiness,[1]
and because this is so,
physical desire,
while rarely self-transcending,
can sometimes be steeped in
compassion and goodness.

For example,
eating a meal of fat beef and spiced wine is a neutral act.
But if done to make your mind
more receptive to the teachings of Torah,[2]
or to honor the Sabbath and festivals,[3]
your intention to serve God elevates the act
and all involved in it in service to God.

(continued on page 25)

4 Talmud, *Pesachim* 117a. Rava was said to punctuate his Torah lessons with humor.

5 Kehot edition, p. 27.

6 *Muttar,* "permitted, released"; a rabbinic category of permitted actions. Because *muttar* means both "permitted" and "released," the Alter Rebbe sees the second meaning as the rationale behind the first.

7 Kehot edition, p. 29.

☰ The inbetweener is not an ascetic. The pleasures of the body are not denied to you. On the contrary, they are there for you to hallow. For example, if eating and drinking are done solely to please the self, their full potential is not realized. When you eat and drink to sustain your life so that you can be of service to God and others, then the act of eating and drinking is hallowed.

This is why permitted actions are called *muttar,* those deeds that release the narrow self into the greater reality of God and godliness. They are not simply permitted but have the potential to unchain you from the constrictive illusion that you and the world you inhabit are separate from God and the universe as a whole.

The same can be said of humor.
If a joke is told to sharpen the mind
and uplift the heart,
it is in service to God.[4, 5]

This what is meant when we say an action is permitted;[6]
it is permitted because it releases the self from the bonds of
    selfishness.[7]

1 The opposite of *muttar* is *assur*, "prohibited, chained"; a rabbinic category of forbidden actions.

2 A sacred commandment; an act of godliness designed to awaken you to God.

3 There are some things so tightly chained to the *sitra achra*, the place of selfishness, that they cannot be hallowed.

4 Kehot edition, p. 31.

8 ☐ Using the Body for Evil

Just as there are permitted actions that free you from the self,
so are there prohibited actions that keep you being chained to
    the self.[1]

Suppose you are tired
and eat to regain the strength
to perform a spiritual deed.[2]

If the food you eat is permitted,
the act of eating elevates the food
by using its energy in godly service.

But if you unwittingly eat a forbidden food,
even the intention of serving God
cannot elevate the food
because the forbidden is held captive to the other side.[3, 4]

What is true regarding
what goes into your mouth
is true regarding what comes out as well.

(continued on page 29)

[5] By using your words more wisely.

[6] *Gehinnom,* or hell, is the world of needless pain and suffering you inhabit when you deliberately set out to harm others.

[7] Kehot edition, p. 33.

[≣] In this and the previous chapter, the Alter Rebbe sets forth three categories of behavior: permitted, forbidden, and neutral. He also introduces the idea of intent. When you do what is permitted or neutral with the intent of gratifying only yourself, the deed never lifts you beyond the self. If, however, you act with the intent of doing something godly, something for the sake of others as well as yourself, then the act hallows the actor and all things involved in that act.

Intent, however, cannot hallow that which is forbidden. The forbidden is forbidden (*assur*) because it chains you to self and selfishness no matter what your intent. And being so chained is what it is to live in hell.

If you engage in innocent chatter
meaning no harm,
but wasting precious breath
on the inconsequential,
you can be cleansed.[5]

But if your speech is deliberately wicked,
if you engage in mockery or slander,
such deeds drag you into hell.[6, 7]

1 *Seichel*, composed of intuitive wisdom, rational understanding, and integrative knowledge (*Chochmah*, *Binah*, and *Da'at*).

2 Ecclesiastes 10:2.

3 Kehot edition, p. 37.

4 Ecclesiastes 9:14.

5 Deuteronomy 6:5.

6 Kehot edition, p. 36.

9 □ The Secret Yearning for the Good

You have two natures,
physical and spiritual,
and each has its own voice.

The physical speaks as
Self-serving passion through
the left side of your heart.

The spiritual speaks as
awakened intellect[1] through
the right side of your heart,
as it is written, "The heart of the wise is on the right."[2, 3]

These two natures battle to control your body
like two armies besieging a city,
for the body is called a "small city."[4]

While the physical resists the spiritual,
the spiritual embraces the physical, as it is written,
"And you shall love *YHVH* your God, with all your heart...."[5, 6]
With all your heart, the left and the right.

(continued on page 33)

7 *Ahavah rabbah,* "infinite love."

8 The evil inclination; the inclination toward selfishness.

9 Psalm 34:14.

10 *Yetzer hara* and *kelipat nogah,* the inclination toward selfishness and the sense of separate self from which it arises and to which it lends support.

11 *Zohar* 2:163a. The *Zohar* tells of a king who hired a prostitute to test the moral character of his son. The woman used all her wiles to seduce the boy, but she harbored in her heart the hope that she would fail. So it is with the inclination toward selfishness (*yetzer hara*): while it focuses on the self, it does so as part of the nonduality (*shlemut*) of God and secretly hopes you will choose a path other than the way of selfishness it is offering you.

12 Kehot edition, p. 39.

☰ There is a battle raging within you between selfishness and selflessness, the inclination toward selfishness (*yetzer hara*) and the inclination toward selflessness (*yetzer hatov*). And while it is possible that "one nation shall prevail over the other nation" (Genesis 25:23), it is not possible for one nation to eradicate the other. The task of the inbetweener is not to defeat the physical but to embrace it in *ahavah rabbah,* infinite and all-consuming love.

Your physical nature, your *yetzer hara* and the shell of self (*kelipat nogah*) that it feeds, is not your enemy. In fact, it wants to be uplifted. It fights hard to be heard because it knows that the true awakening is not at the expense of the physical but through the unification of the spiritual and the physical in the nonduality of God.

This all-encompassing love is called "infinite."[7]
In such love even the inclination toward selfishness[8] is
    redeemed,
for even it desires what it perceives as good,
and when filled with infinite love, it comes to know the true
    good
and so turns away from evil and does good.[9]

Hence even the inclination toward selfishness and the bounded
    separate self[10]
desire to serve God even as they entice you from such service.
In this they are like the seductress of the *Zohar*.[11, 12]

1 *Tzaddikim.*

2 Kehot edition, p. 39.

3 Deuteronomy 21:21.

4 *B'nei aliyah*, those who ascend to the more inclusive levels of intelligence.

5 Shimon ben Yochai, a first-century rabbi (*Tanna*) of the Mishnaic period (70–200 CE), is traditionally thought to be the author of the *Zohar*, the central text of Kabbalah, Jewish mysticism.

6 The Alter Rebbe is paraphrasing the Talmud, *Sukkah* 45b and *Sanhedrin* 97b.

7 Rabbi Chayya was a contemporary of Shimon ben Yochai.

10 □ The Purpose of Transformation

To the completely righteous[1, 2] one can say,
"Eradicate the evil from your midst,"[3]
for they know only good,
and employ the pleasures of the world
solely in service to God.

Such people are called "those who ascend,"[4]
for they lift up even evil to its source in the good.

But do not imagine you are such as they.
As Rabbi Shimon ben Yochai[5] says,
"I have seen the ascending ones, and they are rare."[6]

Even Rabbi Chayya,[7]
who sought the way of ascent, was warned,

(continued on page 37)

8 | *Zohar* 1:4a. Only those who know the unity of opposites in God can achieve this awakening.

9 | Kehot edition, p. 41.

10 | God is both the transcendent One and the immanent many. The transcendent is called the Holy One and is said to be the masculine side of God. The immanent is called *Shechinah*, the Presence of God, and is said to be the feminine side of God.

11 | *Zohar* 2:114b, 3:222b, and 3:288a. The realization of God's nonduality (*shlemut*) is called *da'at devekut*, the awareness of the unity of God, woman, man, and nature.

12 | Kehot edition, p. 43.

☰ | Complete *tzaddikim* are those *b'nei aliyah* who know that there is no darkness without light, or bitterness without sweetness, and who thus see all opposites as manifestations of God. This is *da'at devekut*, the realization that the Holy One and the *Shechinah* are one. The complete *tzaddik* knows this innately, and the inbetweener has to attain it through disciplined practice.

"Only those who can realize darkness as light
and bitter as sweet may enter here."[8, 9]

The purpose of this transformation
is the unification of the transcendent with the immanent[10]
even in the lowest of worlds.[11, 12]

1 *Rasha* is the opposite of the *tzaddik*.

2 Talmud, *Yoma* 86a. The first level of divine forgiveness, reserved for minor offenses of omission, comes immediately at the moment of repentance (*teshuvah*), turning from evil and doing good. The second level of divine forgiveness, reserved for offenses of commission, comes at the conclusion of Yom Kippur, the Day of Atonement. The third level of divine forgiveness, reserved for offenses for which the punishment is *kareit*, exile from the community, comes after a person feels genuine remorse, effects real behavioral change, observes Yom Kippur, and is horrified by the mere idea of *kareit*.

3 Kehot edition, p. 43.

4 Talmud, *Nedarim* 9b. Not all editions of the Talmud contain this phrase.

11 □ Redemption from Evil

The wicked[1] is the antithesis of the righteous,
for the one is obsessed with self
while the other is free from self.
Yet not everyone who succumbs to evil
does so to the same degree.

Some commit minor offenses,
and these only rarely.
And the offenses are followed
by genuine feelings of remorse
and an authentic quest for forgiveness,
at which point they are wicked no longer.

Such a one as this
God forgives you through
one of the three forms of forgiveness.[2, 3]

Even those whose sins are serious
can repent and find forgiveness,
as our Rabbis said,
"The wicked are full of remorse."[4]
These, too, are forgiven.

Yet there are those so wicked,
so imprisoned in self and selfishness,

(continued on page 41)

5 Goodness in this case is called *makkif,* meaning "to surround." The Alter Rebbe is saying that even those who have banished goodness from their hearts are still surrounded by it, and should their hearts break open over another's suffering, goodness will flow in and lead them to redemption. In other words, no one, no matter how evil, is deprived of the opportunity to make repentance (*teshuvah*) and find forgiveness.

6 Kehot edition, p. 45.

Tanya is loathe to condemn anyone or to imagine anyone to be beyond redemption. Indeed, the label *rasha* (wicked) applies only when a person is actively engaged in evil and should not be used to suggest that a person is permanently evil. This is because even "the wicked are full of remorse" (Talmud, *Nedarim* 9b) and surrounded (*makkif*) by goodness.

that goodness cannot penetrate them at all.
Yet even here there is hope,
for goodness surrounds them,
waiting for even the slightest crack
by which it might enter.[5, 6]

[1] The *beinoni* (inbetweener) always struggles with both sides of the heart, the inclination for good and the inclination for evil.

[2] When contemplating the *Sh'ma*, "Hear [*sh'ma*], O Israel, the Infinite is God, the Infinite is One," you surrender to the oneness of God, erasing all sense of separate self.

[3] The *Amidah* (Standing Prayer) is the central prayer of Jewish worship. During the *Amidah*, you stand in the Presence of God and are annulled in that Presence the way a wave is annulled in the ocean.

[4] *Ayn Sof.*

[5] Kehot edition, p. 47.

[6] In *Zohar* 3:224a we are taught that while passions arise of their own accord outside your control, you can choose how to respond to them.

[7] Ecclesiastes 2:13.

[8] Kehot edition, p. 49.

12 □ Bringing Light into the Darkness

Even in the strongest inbetweener
evil is never totally vanquished.[1]
Yet there are times—
especially during the *Sh'ma*[2]
and the *Amidah*[3]—
when you are completely surrendered to God,
your intellect awash in sublime ecstasy,
and emptied in deep contemplation
of the infinite spaciousness of the Endless One.[4]
At such moments evil is overcome and nullified.[5]

When the ecstasy passes,
the selfish passions return,
yet everyone is born with the capacity
to turn these passions Godward,[6]
as it is written,
"Then I saw that wisdom surpasses folly
as light surpasses darkness."[7, 8]

As light effortlessly defeats darkness
and yet cannot erase it,
so the inbetweener defeats evil,
yet negative thoughts continue to arise.

(continued on page 45)

43

9 *Zohar* 1:201a.

10 Kehot edition, p. 51.

≡ An inbetweener is not sometimes good and sometimes evil, but rather forever engaged in bringing selfish passions under the influence of selfless service. While this sounds like a life of inner struggle, the way itself is in fact effortless. Just as a burning candle doesn't struggle against the darkness, but effortlessly keeps it at bay, so you are not to fight your selfish nature, only to kindle the flame of kindness. Refraining from anger and offering kindness to everyone are how you live the way of the inbetweener.

Do not dwell upon such thoughts,
but thrust them aside with both hands,
countering the selfish with the selfless,
refraining from anger
and offering kindness even to those who offend you.[9, 10]

1 Talmud, *Berachot* 61b; the *yetzer hatov* and the *yetzer hara*, the inclination for selfless good and the inclination for selfish evil.

2 The Alter Rebbe deliberately misreads the text to argue that the *beinoni* (inbetweener) judges between competing passions, rather than is judged by them.

3 Kehot edition, p. 53.

4 Talmud, *Kiddushin* 30b.

5 Kehot edition, p. 55.

☰ Since everyone has both good and evil inclinations, there is no sense in being judged by them, but only by how you handle them. The inbetweener lifts the competition to God. This is what is meant by the teaching "I set before you life and death, blessing and curse, therefore choose life that you may live" (Deuteronomy 30:19). If the word "therefore" is a command from God telling us which to choose then there is in fact no choice at all. "Choose life" should not be read as a command, but rather as a consequence. Torah and *Tanya* are saying that if you clearly see that the right side speaks for life and the left side speaks for death, you will naturally "choose life." The real choice is not between life and death, but between seeing and not seeing.

13 □ Internal Conflict

The inbetweener is "judged by both inclinations."[1]
Judged by them,
not *ruled* by them.[2]

The inbetweener listens
to the claims of both inclinations
and judges between them.

When a physical desire arises,
the left side of your heart
is aroused to pursue it.
This is the voice of the inclination toward selfishness.

Bring that passion
into the right side of your heart,
where your intellect
responds with the voice of inclination toward selflessness.[3]

Most often the two inclinations
are in conflict,
so lift the matter to God,
who will strengthen
the goodness of the right,
as our Sages teach,
"Without God's help
the evil inclination
could not be overcome."[4, 5]

[1] Psalm 34:14.

[2] Isaiah 59:2. Sin strengthens your sense of alienation from the whole and excuses exploitation of the other.

[3] Kehot edition, p. 59.

[4] *Nefesh, Ruach,* and *Neshamah*—body, heart, and mind.

[5] The Three Garments.

[6] God, Torah, and *mitzvot.*

[7] Kehot edition, p. 63.

≣ "Your sins stand between you and God" (Isaiah 59:2). Sin arises from selfishness. Selfishness arises from a sense of fear and scarcity. Fear and scarcity arise from the egoic shell of self-isolation (*kelipat nogah*). And this egoic shell arises from *sitra achra*, the other side of God, the side that sees only the many and denies the One and the very possibility of unity.

Because sin can be traced back to *sitra achra*, which is primarily a state of mind, your best defense against sin is the awakened intellect (*seichel*): intuitive wisdom (*Chochmah*), rational understanding (*Binah*), and integrative knowledge (*Da'at*). One way to awaken the intellect is to remind yourself whenever selfish passions arise that they can only lead away from God, when in fact your deepest longing is for union with God. With this in mind, your thoughts will be directed toward God, your words will be words of Torah, and your deeds will be acts of godliness.

14 □ Becoming an Inbetweener

Everyone can attain the level of inbetweener,
and everyone should strive after it.

You can achieve the level of inbetweener at any moment
for it does not require you to despise your passions,
only to control your actions—
to "turn from evil and do good"[1]
in your deeds, speech, and thought.

Whenever a passion arises
that draws you toward evil,
say to yourself,
"This is the way of the wicked
that will separate me from God."[2, 3]
Nothing is worth that separation,
and my deepest wish is to unite
body, heart, and mind[4] with God
by clothing them in thoughts, words, and deeds[5]
dedicated to God, God's will, and God's way.[6, 7]

1 When you return to your divine nature (*penimiyut*), you will see clearly and act godly.

2 Malachi 3:18. Though Malachi is clearly talking about two types of people, the righteous who serve God and the wicked who do not, the Alter Rebbe takes the passage to refer to four kinds of people: the *tzaddik* (righteous), the *rasha* (wicked), the inbetweener who serves God, and the inbetweener who does not.

3 Kehot edition, p. 63.

4 They practice the *mitzvot* simply because it never occurs to them to be otherwise.

15 ☐ Serving God

"And you will return and see[1]
the difference between the righteous and the wicked,
between those who serve God and those who serve God not."[2, 3]

There are two types of inbetweener:
those who serve God
and those who do not serve God.
Those who do not serve God
are not wicked,
but merely passionless,
lacking a sense of self strong enough
to ignite selfish desires or deeds.
They keep the way of God by default,[4]
which is why they are said
not to serve God at all.

The true servant of God
actively arouses love for God.

This can be done in two ways.
First, by immersing the intellect
in the infinite spaciousness of God.

(continued on page 53)

5 Immersing the intellect in the infinite spaciousness (*gadlut*) of the Infinite Godhead (*Ayn Sof*) induces a self-emptying ecstasy (*bittul hayesh*) that engulfs all form (*Yesh*), even the *kelipat nogah* and *sitra achra*, in the emptiness (*Ayn*) of God. The way of self-emptying ecstasy is called perfect or complete because it leaves nothing untouched.

6 Kehot edition, pp. 65–67.

≣ The inbetweener who serves God is a passionate, feeling person who is troubled by the competing voices of the heart and who learns to honor the left side of selfishness by aligning it with the right side of godliness. The alignment comes about in three ways. Some for whom passions are weak conform their actions to the good by adhering strictly to the *mitzvot* (sacred commandments). This is the way of *Nefesh*, the way of doing. Some for whom passions are stronger focus their attention on the heart's innate yearning for God, doing what is right as a lover seeks to please the beloved. This is the way of *Ruach*, the way of feeling. Others for whom passions are strong but who find themselves drawn more to the mind than the heart set their mind to the contemplation of God's infinite spaciousness and in so doing empty themselves completely into the One.

Second, by arousing the passion for God
resting within the right side of the heart.

Both are ways of serving God,
but only the way of immersion
is called perfect service.[5, 6]

1 Intellect (*seichel*) is composed of intuitive wisdom (*Chochmah*), rational understanding (*Binah*), and integrative knowledge (*Da'at*).

2 Doing justly, loving mercy, and walking humbly (Micah 6:8).

3 *Tevunah* is an intellectual understanding of God's nonduality that engages the self without emptying the self.

4 Talmud, *Kiddushin* 40a.

5 Kehot edition, pp. 67–69.

≡ The experience of union in, with, and as God triggers a bliss so intense as to temporarily erase your very sense of self: your sense of independence (*Neshamah*) is absorbed into the larger sense of inter-dependence (*Chayyah*), and both dissolve into the nonduality of God as the only true reality (*Yechidah*). Yet not everyone is comfortable with this goal, and for those who are not, there is a lesser but still profound awakening called *tevunah*, "comprehension." *Tevunah* is the "good thought," the thought of God's nonduality (*shlemut*), that, no less than ecstatic union, aligns your actions with godliness.

Imagine two people listening to a great symphony. One is lost in the exquisite beauty of the sound, oblivious to self. The other, visual-izing the score in her mind, is no less awed yet in no way lost. The first is experiencing *bittul hayesh*, the emptying of all things into *Ayn*, the Nothing. The second is experiencing *tevunah*, intellectual rapture. *Bit-tul* is superior to *tevunah*, but both align you with God and godliness.

16 □ The Essential Task

The essential task
of those who serve God
is to surrender the selfish passions
to the divine light of intellect[1]
by meditating on the spaciousness of God.

Contemplating God's spaciousness
stokes the love of God
in the right side of your heart,
enflaming a yearning for God
so strong as to align
all your deeds with godliness.[2]

If such passion is alien to you,
do not despair,
for you can love God rationally
even if you do not do so emotionally.

Such love is called comprehension or
the intellectual love of God,[3]
and it too aligns your deeds
with godliness,
as our Sages taught,
"The Holy One, blessed be He,
joins a good thought to the deed."[4, 5]

[1] *Tevunah*.

[2] Deuteronomy 30:14. The Alter Rebbe will refer to this verse again and again, parsing it to reveal deeper and deeper layers of truth.

[3] Kehot edition, p. 71.

[4] Talmud, *Berachot* 18b. The wicked are considered dead even in life, for their actions serve only themselves.

17 □ The Practice of Comprehension

Loving God intellectually,[1]
you can understand the verse,
"For this thing is very near to you,
in your mouth and in your heart,
that you may do it."[2, 3]

The "it" is *tevunah*, the rational love of God,
for while ecstasy is not for everyone,
reason is.
You can contemplate God's infinity
at any time, and when you do
you will generate at least this rational love
that leads to godly action.

This is true even for the wicked,
whose deeds give no life,[4]
for rational love can shatter
the iron wall that separates them from God.

(continued on page 59)

5 Goodness surrounds (*makkif*) the heart like the sea surrounds the hull of a ship. If the hull should crack, the sea rushes in. It is the same with the heart and goodness.

6 Psalm 51:19.

7 Kehot edition, p. 73.

≣ Again we find the Alter Rebbe refusing to write off even the wicked, for everyone is a manifestation of God and can awaken to God. If this is so, then awakening is neither esoteric nor difficult to achieve. On the contrary, it is "in your mouth and in your heart, that you may do it" (Deuteronomy 30:14). In other words, every person, no matter how alienated from God and others he or she may feel himself or herself to be, is innately capable of shattering the iron wall of separation (*kelipat nogah*). How? Through the cultivation of the intellect (*seichel*).

When you devote your mind to contemplating the infinite expanse of God, you begin to realize that you are a part of That. Understanding that God's *ahavah rabbah*, God's infinite love, must embrace even the most alienated and lost, you begin to doubt the absoluteness of your alienation. The iron wall you imagined separating you from God begins to crack. And when it does, goodness seeps in, slowly hollowing out the *kelipah nogah* so that it becomes more and more transparent to the light of God.

Why? Because even rational love
leads to remorse,
and remorse to a broken heart,
and a broken heart to goodness,[5]
as it is written,
"The sacrifices to God are
a broken spirit,
a broken and contrite heart."[6, 7]

1 Deuteronomy 30:14.

2 *Bittul.*

3 *Tevunah.*

4 Everything from quarks to quasars has its own level of consciousness, its own innate wisdom and intelligence.

5 Proverbs 3:19.

6 Psalm 104:24.

7 Ecclesiastes 7:12. The Alter Rebbe is reading this text unconventionally. Rather than assume the "it" that is possessed is, as the text clearly intends, "wisdom," he assumes it refers to "life." In this way the text reads, "Wisdom gives life to all the living." Wisdom is the life force itself.

8 The Alter Rebbe is playing with the word *chochmah*, "wisdom," defining it as the capacity to know the essence (*choch*) of what is (*mah*). That essence is God.

18 □ The Nature of Wisdom

"For this thing is very near to you."[1]
What is this thing that is very near?

For some it may be self-emptying,[2]
and for others it may be rational love,[3]
but these still require a level of effort and practice
that may not be available to everyone.
The "it" that is near must be near to all.
And this "it" is wisdom,
for wisdom rests within all things,[4]
as it is written,
"God founded the earth in wisdom,"[5] and
"In wisdom You have made them all."[6]

Further, wisdom fills all life, as it is written,
"Wisdom gives life to those who possess it."[7]

Wisdom is the capacity
to intuit the essence of all things;[8]
the faculty by which you glimpse
the true nature of what is.

And what is, is God,
and wisdom reveals the Presence of God
even to the most foolish

(continued on page 63)

9 Psalm 73:22–23. No matter how foolish or ignorant you are, even if you act in a manner that denies your humanity, still God is with you, and the wisdom to know God and act godly is never lost to you.

10 Kehot edition, p. 75.

≣ The promise of the *Tanya* is that anyone can awaken to God as the source and substance of all reality and in so doing "turn from evil and do good." This promise is rooted in the idea that all people are innately capable of intuiting the unity of God manifest as the multiplicity of creation. This capability is called *Chochmah*, "wisdom."

Chochmah is the first of the Three Mothers, the three faculties (along with rational understanding and integrative knowledge) that compose your intellect (*seichel*). *Chochmah* is not reserved for the righteous but is given freely to all, even the foolish and inhumane. The challenge is not to earn wisdom, but to access the wisdom already inside you.

and ignorant,
as it is written,
"I am foolish and ignorant,
I am as a beast before You—
and I am constantly with You."[9, 10]

1 Proverbs 20:27. *Neshamah* is the egoic consciousness that perceives itself as a separate self.

2 The body.

3 Kehot edition, p. 77.

4 *Nefesh* (bodily intelligence) and *Ruach* (emotional intelligence).

5 Genesis 25:30.

6 Talmud, *Berachot* 18b.

7 Job 4:21.

8 Kehot edition, p. 79.

9 Ecclesiastes 7:12.

10 Psalm 78:65.

19 □ The Candle of God

"The self is a candle of God."[1]

The self is a flickering flame,
striving to separate itself from the wick.[2, 3]

Despite all its attachments
to matter and mood,[4]
once awake to wisdom
the self yearns to abandon itself
and be emptied into God.

Self and selfishness cry, "Feed me!"[5]
Yet even when fed they are called "dead,"[6]
for they "die without wisdom."[7, 8]

Wisdom "gives life"[9]
and rests even in the wicked.
Though hidden from them
by their obsession with the self,
wisdom can be found, as it is written,
"Then God awakened as one out of sleep."[10]

(continued on page 67)

11   Isaiah 40:17.

12   Psalm 68:3.

13   Kehot edition, p. 81.

≣   God embraces all reality. Even *Neshamah*, the ego insisting it is apart from, rather than a part of, God, is not left behind. Indeed, God manifests as seemingly separate selves in order to shine the light of unity in the world of diversity. The true purpose of *Neshamah* is to become a flame of God illuminating the Presence of God in and as all seemingly separate things.

Yet do not imagine, as often the newly awakened *Neshamah* does, that God is on one side rather than the other (*sitra achra*), or that God is other than the shells of self (*kelipot*), the needs of the body (*Nefesh*), or the passions of the heart (*Ruach*). God is all of this. And the *Neshamah* must feed them. But the awakened *Neshamah* must feed them with wisdom; that is, it must uplift the physical and emotional dimensions of life in service to the whole.

The awakening of God
is the waking to God through wisdom.
At that moment all shells become transparent,
as it is written, "All nations are as nothing before God,"[11]
and evil dissolves "as wax melts before a flame."[12, 13]

[1] From the daily morning liturgy.

[2] Malachi 3:6.

[3] Kehot edition, p. 83.

[4] Psalm 33:6.

[5] Kehot edition, p. 85.

[≣] At issue here is the tension between ever-changing form (*Yesh*) and unchanging emptiness (*Ayn*). If God and world were separate, there would be no tension: God would be the unchanging, and the world would be the ever-changing. The issue would then be how the unchanging God creates and continues to remain relevant to the ever-changing world. But this kind of dualistic theology is anathema to *Tanya*. There can be only one reality, and that is God, the Infinite (*Ayn Sof*) that embraces and transcends the finite.

The theology of *Tanya* is nondual; that is, the One and the many have to be reconciled in a greater Whole. This is done by envisioning God as dynamic rather than static. God does not change from one thing to another; God is change that makes one thing and another.

Think in terms of the relationship between ocean and wave. The ocean is no less ocean for all its waves. Just as the ocean is always ocean even as it swirls and crests and raises infinite waves, so God is always God even as God manifests the myriad forms of creation. And just as waves are no less real for being nothing other than the temporary swelling of the ocean, so creation is no less real for being the temporary forms of God.

With this analogy in mind, we can better understand the Alter Rebbe's analogy to breath and words. As the ocean fills each wave, so breath fills each word. As the ocean withdraws back into itself, bringing with it the end of that wave, so breath fades and the word falls silent.

20 ☐ The Unchanging One

God is One and Unique,
unchanging and without end,
as it is written,
"You are God before creation,
and You are God after creation,"[1]
and "I, *YHVH*, have not changed."[2, 3]

God is the one Life
present in all life,
as breath is present in every word.

Just as the word is the garment of breath,
so creation is the "breath of His mouth."[4, 5]

1 *Tikkunei Zohar, Tikkun 57*, p. 91b.

2 Kehot edition, p. 87.

3 Psalm 139:12.

4 *Kelipot.*

5 Deuteronomy 4:35. *YHVH*, the four-letter Hebrew Name of God, represents the transcendent, and *Elohim* represents the immanent. *Tanya* is saying that God is God from the most sublime to the most mundane levels, from emptiness (*Ayn*) to form (*Yesh*).

6 Kehot edition, p. 89.

≣ Nothing is outside of God; indeed, there is no "outside" at all.

If there is nothing separate from God, if *no place is empty of God* (*Tikkunei Zohar* 57, p. 91b), why do we feel ourselves to be separate? This is the nature of God's nonduality (*shlemut*). God cannot be limited to either emptiness (*Ayn*) or form (*Yesh*). God as the Infinite (*Ayn Sof*) must embrace and transcend them both. The mistake we make is to imagine that the form is somehow other than God and that the shells that blind us to God are somehow evil and in need of removal.

From *Tanya's* perspective, the shells are as natural to God as a turtle's shell is to the turtle. The task of the inbetweener isn't to remove the shells but to see them as part of God as well. This is what *Chochmah*, wisdom, knows, for it reveals the divine suchness (*choch*) in all that is (*mah*). Realizing this is realizing that *YHVH* is *Elohim* (Deuteronomy 4:35). *Elohim* is a plural noun meaning "gods." The plurality designates God's presence in the plurality of the world of form (*Yesh*). *Elohim* is the One manifest as the many. *YHVH* is singular, referring to the transcendent One in and of Itself. *YHVH* refers to God's essential unity.

21 □ God's Speech

God's speech is not like your speech.
When you utter a word,
the word seems outside of you.
But there is nothing outside of God,
and "no place is empty of Him."[1, 2]

Even when God speaks and words become worlds,
the absolute union of God and creation is unbroken,
and hence God has not changed.

As breath is veiled in sound,
becoming word to a listener,
so God's light is veiled in form,
becoming creation to the created.

God perceives no other,
for everything is God without distinction.
This is what is meant when it is written
that darkness and light are the same to God.[3]

Even the shells of self[4] are not other than God,
just as a turtle's shell is not other than the turtle.
Thus it is written, "*YHVH* is *Elohim*."[5, 6]

[1] Talmud, *Berachot* 31b.

[2] Kehot edition, p. 89.

[3] *Adam Kadmon, Atzilut, Beriah, Yetzirah,* and *Assiyah*—spirit, soul, mind, heart, and body.

[4] *Kelipot* and *sitra achra.*

[5] Kehot edition, p. 91.

[6] Isaiah 47:8; Zephaniah 2:15.

[7] Talmud, *Sotah* 4b.

[8] Kehot edition, p. 93.

☰ Your very existence depends on your capacity to say "I am." *Neshamah* is the faculty that allows this to happen. Since God's non-duality (*shlemut*) necessitates the existence of a multiplicity of "I am," it would be a mistake to imagine that *Neshamah* is evil or that it must be eliminated. The same is true of the *kelipot*, the shells that allow you to see objects as other than yourself, and the *kelipat nogah*, the shell of ego, which allows you to be you at all. Everything, from the most sublime to the most mundane, is part of God's infinite creativity.

The problem is not with the *Neshamah* and *kelipot* themselves, but with our ignorance. The problem is not that you say, "I am," but that you mistakenly assume "there is nothing besides me." This ignorance is maintained by ignoring the fact that you cannot exist alone, that you are not separate from your environment, and that the whole environment, from *Adam Kadmon* to *Assiyah* (the first and fifth worlds of divine emanation), is the outpouring of God's creativity.

22 □ Other Gods

"Torah speaks as humans speak,"[1]
giving the impression of duality.[2]
But there is no duality in God,
and the one Light animates all worlds,[3]
including even those mired in self and otherness.[4]

Unawakened selves are called "other gods,"
their otherness falsely derived
from their imagined distance from God.[5]

Perceiving nothing but themselves,
they proclaim themselves gods, saying,
"I am, and there is nothing besides me."[6]

Thus arrogance is the heart of idolatry.[7]
But arrogance is rooted in delusion,
for there is nothing but God.[8]

1 *Zohar* 1:24a; *Zohar* 2:60a.

2 *Mitzvot*, those sacred commandments designed to awaken you to the *Shechinah*, the infinite Presence of God.

3 *Tikkunei Zohar, Tikkun* 30.

4 *Tzedakah*.

5 Kehot edition, p. 93.

6 *Pirke Avot* 3:17.

7 Kehot edition, p. 99.

☰ An inbetweener continually recalls her unity with God and her obligations to godliness. One way to do this is through Torah, not simply the study of Torah but through the living of Torah. The ultimate challenge of Torah is to "be holy as I *YHVH* am holy" (Leviticus 19:2). The only way we can be as God is, is if we are what God is, and this is what *Tanya* tells us over and again: God is the All in all. Knowing this, we engage the world justly, kindly, and humbly (Micah 6:8). Torah is a way for us to discover who we are and what we are to do.

This is not done didactically. Torah study is not about gathering information; it is about generating awe. Torah reveals the unity of God, woman, man, and nature, and this revelation triggers an overwhelming awe that in turn awakens *Chochmah*, our intuitive wisdom aware of God's nonduality.

While everyone can study Torah, not everyone has this capacity for awe. Such people should focus on living Torah through the *mitzvot* and in this way discovering awe through action.

23 □ Torah and God Are One

"Torah and God are entirely one."[1]
Thus when you are engaged in Torah,
both through study and spiritual practice,[2]
you and God are one.

Engaging in spiritual practice represents God's innermost will,
and the practices are called the "organs of the King."[3]
When you engage in such practice
you become an organ of divine will.
Thus when your hand distributes funds to the poor,[4, 5]
it becomes the hand of God
and a vehicle of godliness.

Study of Torah arouses great awe,
great awe arouses sublime wisdom,
and sublime wisdom reveals
your unity with God,
as our Sages said,
"If there is no wisdom
there is no awe."[6]

You may not immediately achieve such awe,
yet even so, do not abandon the practices,
for they can transform you over time.[7]

1 *Sitra achra.*

2 Kehot edition, p. 99.

3 The *kelipot*, the shells of separateness and independent selfhood, are part of God's nonduality (*shlemut*). They are simply God manifesting diversity to balance God manifesting unity.

4 Numbers 22:18. The prophet Bilaam was sent by the enemies of Israel to curse the Israelites but could not violate God's will and actually do so.

5 People can be so ignorant of God's nonduality as to imagine themselves truly separate from God. This level of ignorance is called "folly."

6 Talmud, *Sotah* 3a.

7 Kehot edition, p. 101.

≣ God's will and God's nature are one and the same. What God wills is to be God. To be God means to manifest the myriad potentialities of life in all five worlds and levels of consciousness. Thus it is no less God's will to manifest *Neshamah* and its sense of independence as it is to manifest *Chayyah* and its sense of interdependence. God cannot be limited to those things we call spiritual (light, peace, goodness, selflessness, etc.) and must include the other side, the *sitra achra* (darkness, conflict, evil, selfishness, etc.). This is what we call God's nonduality (*shlemut*).

God does not choose between opposites. There is no choice in God. God cannot choose to be other than God, and therefore God cannot choose to be other than the Whole. Created in the image and likeness of God, you, too, contain opposites. Your task is not to eliminate one side or the other, but to lift both in service to the Whole. This means overcoming the ignorance of separateness in a way that allows the self to be for itself and others at the same time. This is the teaching of Hillel, who said, "If I am not for myself, who will be for me? If I am only for myself, what [good] am I? And if not now, when?" (*Pirke Avot* 1:14).

24 □ The Interplay of Opposites

Creation is the interplay of opposites.
The highest realm of godliness
is balanced by the "other side" of selfishness,[1]
and just as the first reveals unity,
the latter reveals diversity.[2]

Do not mistake opposites for enemies.
The self is not in rebellion against God,[3]
but actually serves God.
Just as Bilaam says, "I cannot violate the word of God,"[4]
so the self cannot violate the will of God.

Yet human ignorance can be so great
as to allow for the illusion of rebellion against God
rooted in the folly of separation from God.[5]

This is why our Sages say,
"No one commits any sin
unless a spirit of folly enters into him."[6, 7]

1 Deuteronomy 30:14.

2 Kehot edition, p. 105.

3 Talmud, *Yoma* 85b.

4 Jerusalem Talmud, *Pe'ah* 1:1.

5 Kehot edition, p. 107.

≣ "For this thing is very near to you" (Deuteronomy 30:14). In this reading of the text, the Alter Rebbe defines "this thing" as the innate love of God resting in your heart, just as he earlier spoke of God's love surrounding your heart. By arousing this love you recall your divine nature (*penimiyut*) and achieve realization of your continual union with God (*da'at devekut*).

Anyone can do this, because no one is beyond redemption. Yet some might object and point to the Sages, who taught, "One who says: 'I will sin and then repent, and then sin and repent again,' is not given the opportunity to do so" (Talmud, *Yoma* 85b). Yet the Alter Rebbe refuses to write off anyone and insists that even the habit of sin can be broken if you wish to break it. Thus he reminds us, "Nothing can stand in the way of repentance" (Jerusalem Talmud, *Pe'ah* 1:1).

The Hebrew for "repentance," *teshuvah*, means "to turn." The inbetweener turns from evil to do good, turns from selfishness to selflessness, turns from the folly of separation to the wisdom of union. And then turns again. The turning isn't once and for all, but over and again, for the spirit of folly continually haunts the *Neshamah*, and you must continually turn toward godliness.

25 □ Folly

Here is another meaning of the teaching
"For this thing is very near to you."[1]

Even when folly enters into you,
you can be free of it.

Folly causes you to forget your unity with God.
Remembering unity erases folly.
You remember your union with God
by arousing the love of God
that is always present in your heart.[2]

Even if folly leads to idolatry,
still you can turn from it and be free.

True, our Sages said,
"One who says, 'I will sin and repent,
and sin and repent again,'
is not given an opportunity to repent."[3]
But this does not mean that repentance is denied them,
only that God will not provide them
with an opportunity to repent.
They must seize their own moment for repentance,
and then God will forgive them, for, as it is written,
"Nothing can stand in the way of repentance."[4, 5]

[1] Proverbs 14:23.

[2] Psalm 51:19.

[3] Kehot edition, p. 111.

[4] Psalm 51:10. You cannot hear joy unless and until you are capable of hearing sadness; you cannot hear gladness unless and until you are capable of hearing suffering.

[5] Talmud, *Berachot* 9:5.

26 □ The Profit of Sadness

"In every sadness there will be profit."[1]

What is the profit in sadness?
A broken heart shatters the self
and the glittering shell of selfishness
that seems to separate you from God.

"A broken spirit, a broken heart …
You will not despise."[2, 3]

When your heart is broken
over the suffering you have caused,
your sense of otherness is shattered,
and you can no longer ignore the suffering of others,
and you are able to "hear joy and gladness."[4]

"Just as you recite a blessing for good fortune
so you must recite a blessing for misfortune."[5]
Why?
Because your suffering

(continued on page 83)

6   Psalm 91:1.

7   Kehot edition, p. 113.

≣   The way of awe through Torah is not for everyone, nor is the way of *mitzvot*, spiritual practice. So the Alter Rebbe offers yet another path, the way of the broken heart.

The heart conditioned by the isolation of the *sitra achra* (the other side of God that denies your connection with God) is encased in *kelipah nogah*, the glittering shell of selfishness. Such a heart is hard yet also brittle. It loves what it loves for its own ends, and because it loves this way, it often causes needless suffering that ultimately destroys what it loves. When love is lost there is heartbreak, a moment of sadness so sharp as to crack the shell of selfishness.

When the shell is cracked, you experience the suffering of others, and because you experience the suffering of others, you connect with them. This connection is the voice of joy and gladness. Hence even a moment of great sadness can be a moment of greater transformation, for in that sadness the self recognizes its interconnection with the other. In this way God-realization (*da'at devekut*) is the secret profit in even the most terrible suffering.

attunes you to the suffering of others,
and being so attuned breaks your heart,
allowing the light of God to pierce
the iron ball of isolated self.

Hence it is written,
"The Most High abides in secrecy."[6, 7]

[1] Numbers 15:39.

[2] Talmud, *Kiddushin* 39b.

[3] Kehot edition, p. 115.

27 □ Passive Restraint

Not all sadness arises from a broken heart.
Perhaps your sadness stems from
haunting negative thoughts and desires.

Do not despair over such thoughts,
for every illicit thought
provides an opportunity for turning
and in so doing to fulfill the commandment
"You shall not follow after your heart
and after your eyes,
by which you go astray."[1]

Our Sages taught,
"When you passively refrain from sin,
you are rewarded as though
you had actively performed a commandment."[2, 3]

Do not despair over such thoughts
even if they arise in you all day long,
for perhaps subduing such thoughts
is the reason why you were created.

(continued on page 87)

4   Talmud, *Bava Batra* 16a.

5   Kehot edition, p. 117.

6   Leviticus 20:7.

7   Kehot edition, p. 119.

The Alter Rebbe imagines yet another kind of inbetweener, the person who suffers not from impure deeds, but from impure thoughts. Again do not despair, for these thoughts are themselves opportunities for turning.

Rather than seek to eliminate such thoughts from your mind, which in fact only focuses your attention on them all the more strongly, all you need to do is not follow after them (Numbers 15:39). When these thoughts arise, simply turn your attention to something else. Our Sages call this passive resistance, and about it they say, "When you passively refrain from sin, you are rewarded as if you had actually performed a *mitzvah*" (Talmud, *Kiddushin* 39b). To passively refrain is to consciously allow a thought to pass by without attending to it. Not following a thought allows it to fade from consciousness.

Rather than despair over the wickedness in your mind, entertain the possibility that this is why you were created in the first place. Dealing with such thoughts is your spiritual path. Even if you spend your entire life shifting attention from bad thoughts to good, rejoice, for this is the work you have been given, and in time it, too, will lead to God-realization (*da'at devekut*).

This is what Job meant when he said to God, "You have created the wicked" (Talmud, *Bava Batra* 16a). Job did not mean that God created humankind to be wicked, but that God created wicked thoughts to provide those who think them with an opportunity to turn from them.

About this Job said to God,
"You have created the wicked."[4, 5]
This means that God created
wicked thoughts that you might
subdue them by averting your mind from them
and in this way "sanctify yourselves, and be holy."[6, 7]

[1] Every evil thought has its root in something good. Lust, for example, arises from love, and anger from the desire for justice. The righteous person (*tzaddik*) has the power to trace an evil thought to its root and in this way transform it into something good. This practice requires a level of mental control that few possess, and the Alter Rebbe does not advise you to engage in this practice.

[2] Kehot edition, p. 121.

[3] Proverbs 26:4. Fighting thoughts with thoughts only strengthens the distraction.

[4] Kehot edition, p. 123.

28 □ Distracting Thoughts

Evil thoughts can even arise
during study and prayer,
and if they do,
you should ignore them entirely
and avert your mind from them immediately.

Do not try to examine these thoughts,
for that is a task for the righteous
in whom evil finds no root.[1]
But the evil you experience
is rooted in your own selfishness.

Do not be dejected because of this,
rather redouble your efforts
to concentrate your mind
and in this way
fill yourself with joy and gladness,
realizing that distractions arise
because your prayer and study
are approaching selflessness.[2]

When distractions arise, ignore them, and
"answer not fools according to their folly,
lest you too become a fool."[3, 4]

(continued on page 91)

5 Psalm 124:5.

≣ It is one thing to be distracted by negative thoughts during regular moments of the day, but what if they occur during times specifically devoted to spiritual practice? Does this mean that you are failing in your practice? Not all. In fact, it means just the opposite. Our Sages taught, "The greater the person, the greater the *yetzer hara* [evil inclination]" (Talmud, *Sukkah* 52a); that is, the *yetzer hatov* (good inclination) is always balanced by the *yetzer hara,* and you cannot escape from one to the other. This is why few sinners are beyond redemption, and few saints are beyond temptation.

The challenge is not to eliminate the negative thinking but to deal with it effectively. For the righteous, the best way to deal with such thoughts is to examine them thoroughly and in so doing to discover that they too are part of the divine nonduality (*shlemut*). For the inbetweener, however, such examination may result in becoming obsessed with such thoughts; hence, the best way for the inbetweener to deal with the negative thoughts is to let them go. Do not feed them either by resisting them or by entertaining them. If they come, let them go.

Yet there may be times when you cannot ignore the madness in your mind. Even then the thoughts can be useful, for they remind you of your limitations and humble you to the point where all you can do is cry out to God. And that act of complete humbling is often enough to awaken you to your true nature as a manifestation of God.

What if you cannot ignore them?
Then humble yourself before God
and ask God to rescue you
from these "turbulent waters."[5]

[1] *Timtum halev*, "a dull heart," a heart numb to all feeling.

[2] Kehot edition, p. 123.

[3] The *Zohar* (Book of Splendor) was written in thirteenth-century Spain by rabbi and mystic Moses de Leon. A mystical commentary on the Bible, the *Zohar* is the foundation text of medieval Jewish Kabbalah.

[4] *Zohar* 3:168a. Some obstacles are simply too great to be taken on directly; they need to be broken up into smaller, more manageable pieces. This is true of a dull heart. You cannot simply will your heart to feel, but must arouse it slowly, bit by bit, by changing those thoughts, words, and deeds that dull the heart in the first place.

[5] Kehot edition, p. 127.

[6] Psalm 4:5.

[7] Talmud, *Berachot* 5a. This doesn't mean that you will pit good against evil, but that you will realize that just as evil grows to match the good, so now good will grow to balance the evil.

[8] Kehot edition, p. 129.

29 □ A Dull Heart

Just as an active and distracting mind
is one challenge,
a dull and lifeless heart is another.[1, 2]

To arouse a dull heart,
follow the advice of the holy *Zohar*,[3]
"A wooden beam that does not burn
should be splintered,
and a body opaque to light
should be crushed."[4, 5]

How is this done?
By observing the foolishness in your
thoughts, words, deeds, and dreams.
And by reading the lives
and teachings of saints.

In this way you will
"tremble and sin not,"[6]
that is, you will
"rouse the good against the evil."[7, 8]

In this way you discover that
the other side also serves God;

(continued on page 95)

9 Kehot edition, p. 131.

▤ *Timtum halev*, "dullness of heart," is more troubling than even the glittering ball of selfishness, the *kelipat nogah*, at its most thick and alienated. At least the *kelipah nogah* could feel heartbreak and through this break open to the heartbreak of others and the unity of self and other in God. The dull heart feels nothing. It has to be made to feel, and for this it must be "splintered" and "crushed" (*Zohar* 3:168a).

You do this by comparing your thoughts, words, deeds, and even dreams to those of spiritual giants. This will awaken a sense of trembling; you will be shocked by the lifelessness that has entrapped you, by how far you have fallen into the despair of the *sitra achra*, the "other side," that aspect of you that falls prey to selfishness and alienation. And this sense of horror will, in fact, awaken your innate sense of goodness, the *yetzer hatov*.

In this way you will come to value the "other side" as yet another gift from God, for without the harrowing darkness there is no value to the hallowing light.

Just as *yetzer hatov* balances *yetzer hara*, so light balances darkness. Each goes with the other, and together they partake of the non-duality of God. God manifests as the other side (*sitra achra*) and the shells of self (*kelipot*) in order to provide you with the dark against which the light can shine and be known. God gives rise to foolishness that you might discover wisdom. God allows for dullness that you might tremble with life. Everything is as it is to provide you with the opportunity to see What Is.

offering you another way
to awaken to your unity with God.
It is merely being granted permission
to confuse you with false and deceitful words,
in order that you may be more richly rewarded.[9]

1 *Timtum halev.*

2 *Pirke Avot* 4:10.

3 *Pirke Avot* 2:4.

4 Hosea 7:6.

5 Kehot edition, p. 133.

6 Kehot edition, p. 135.

≣ Those who suffer from *timtum halev*, "dullness of heart," cannot address their situation directly. They cannot simply rouse themselves to love of God or neighbor, for dull hearts lack this kind of passion. The temptation of *timtum halev* is to deny how dull your heart is by focusing on the sins of others.

The dull of heart rarely sin. They simply lack the energy to do so. Their error is to mistake the absence of temptation as a sign that they have defeated their evil inclination (*yetzer hara*). They see the struggles of others to resist temptations and imagine themselves to be morally and spiritually superior. Their pride masks their dullness and excuses their lack of spiritual maturation.

The Alter Rebbe's antidote to dullness of heart is to cultivate true humility by imagining yourself in the place of those for whom temptation is a serious challenge. In other words, he wants you to use your imagination to set your evil inclination ablaze "like a flaming fire" (Hosea 7:6).

This may sound counterintuitive: isn't the evil inclination our enemy? No! On the contrary, the evil inclination, properly understood and employed, is the catalyst for *teshuvah*, returning to God and godliness. The desire of the inclination is not for evil, but to arouse your compassion for self and others by awakening you to the presence of evil and the suffering evil causes when it isn't yoked to the inclination for good (*yetzer hatov*). Placing yourself in the shoes of others awakens you to your limitations even as it humbles you in the face of theirs.

30 □ Cultivating Humility

Moving through dullness of heart[1]
requires you to work with it
rather than against it.

Working with it, you must
"be humble before everyone."[2]
Being humble, you must not
"judge others until you
stand in their place."[3]

There are those whose situation
surrounds them with illicit delights
and places them in constant temptation.
And there are those in whom
temptation "burns like a flaming fire."[4, 5]

You cannot know
the fierceness of their struggle
to resist temptation,
for the inclination toward evil is unique to each of us.

Therefore weigh and examine your own place,
and measure your own capacity to pass this test.[6]

1 *Atzvut,* "depression."

2 *Kelipat nogah.*

3 The spark of God is always spoken of as feminine, as are the five levels of intelligence and the Presence of God Herself, the *Shechinah.* This is to balance the masculine language of God and prevent any idolatrous limitations of God as being male or female.

31 □ Working with Sadness

As you arouse your heart
by facing your inclination toward evil
you may find yourself
engulfed in a deep and troubling sadness.[1]
If so, do not be alarmed.

Such sadness arises from
and operates within
the shell of self,[2]
yet it draws energy from
your innate yet hidden desire
for God and godliness
and thus kindles your
passion for self-transformation.

To work with sadness, say to yourself:
"I feel utterly removed from God,
yet within me is the light of God
desiring only to return to God.

"Let me return this spark
to her father's house,[3]
where she is united with God as God.
Therefore I will cry out to God,

(continued on page 101)

4 When you admit you are alienated from God, you are also admitting that you know you are alienated from God, and this knowing can only come from a place that is not alienated. Hence, the feeling of alienation stems from a source of integration; shift your attention to that source and in time the sadness will be transformed.

5 *Teshuvah* through *maasim tovim*, literally "returning through good deeds." *Teshuvah* is often translated as "repentance," but its literal meaning, "turning" or "returning," is far more revealing. "Repent" means to feel remorse, but *teshuvah* means to use that feeling of remorse to return to God and godliness. The way of returning to God is through acts of godliness, *maasim tovim*, especially acts of selfless kindness.

6 Talmud, *Shabbat* 153a.

7 Kehot edition, pp. 139–141.

≡ Rabbi Schneur Zalman knows the seductive power of sadness to excuse inaction and spiritual sloth. He also knows that to decry sadness, or to insist that you overcome it, is simply to strengthen your sense of powerlessness. If you could stop being sad or brokenhearted, you would; but you can't. Insisting that you should is simply silly.

The Alter Rebbe is far too wise to allow sadness to keep you from spiritual maturation. Rather than claim sadness as a block that must be removed, he sees it as yet another tool to be used. You're sad and despairing of your ability to overcome selfishness and realize your true nature as a part of God? Good! That very despair can be a doorway to *teshuvah,* return!

Working with depression (*atzvut*) begins with the imagination. Imagine the light of God trapped within the shell of ego. She longs to return home to her source, but your obsession with self prevents this. Feel her pain, her suffering, her longing. This is the deeper *atzvut,* the deeper heartbreak, that will arouse you to be her liberator. How? Through *maasim tovim,* selfless acts of kindness toward others.

and God will end this captivity
and reunite her with Himself."[4]

This is the practice known as
returning through kindness.[5]
It should occupy you all your life.[6, 7]

1 *Maasim tovim.*

2 Leviticus 19:18.

3 Talmud, *Shabbat* 31a. According to the Talmud, a gentile once approached Rabbi Hillel demanding that he teach him the entire Torah while standing on one foot. Hillel met the man's challenge saying, "What is hateful to you, do not do to another. This is the entire Torah. All the rest is commentary. Now go and study it!"

4 Kehot edition, p. 145.

☰ Performing selfless acts of kindness (*maasim tovim*) is a direct path to God-realization, for it reveals the unity of self and other in, with, and as God. This is the meaning hidden in the command to "love your neighbor as yourself" (Leviticus 19:18).

Torah doesn't say, "Love your neighbor as you *love* yourself," for this puts the focus on love. You may or may not love yourself, and even if you do, the self you love is most likely the egoic self of *Neshamah* consciousness that sees itself forever separate from your neighbor. *Neshamah* cannot love anything as part of itself, since the entire purpose of *Neshamah* is to maintain the illusion of a separate self.

Loving another as yourself moves you beyond self to soul, beyond the isolated ego (*Neshamah*) that sees self and other as apart from God, to the integrated soul (*Chayyah*) that sees self and other as a part of God. This is why our Sages say that turning from self to soul cannot happen in "an imperfect place" (*Zohar* 1:216b), that is, a place of fragmentation. Turning happens when the fragmented self meets the integrated soul. While it is the fragmented self that is turned (toward wholeness), the turning itself happens in the soul.

32 □ Love Your Neighbor

To practice acts of kindness[1]
is to "love your neighbor as yourself."[2]

Loving your neighbor as yourself
reveals the unity of neighbor and self,
for no one is separate from another,
and all beings are equal,
having a single source
in the One who is all.

This explains Hillel's teaching,
"This is the entire Torah;
the rest is commentary."[3]

Torah's sole purpose
is to remove the veils of diversity
to reveal the divine unity,
that you might then
love the One by loving the many.[4]

1 The realization of God in, with, and as all things manifests as indescribable joy. Joy is not the same as happiness, and it is important that you do not mistake the two. Happiness comes and goes dependent upon the circumstances of the moment, but joy is a deeper sense of the sublime that is sustained regardless of circumstance.

2 God is infinite, unbounded. To say that one thing is God while another is not, is to place a limit on God that reduces God to god. We are in the habit of saying God is in heaven, or God is in me, but the greater truth is that heaven and earth, you and all creation, are in God and of God, the same way a wave is in the ocean, of the ocean.

3 This is a fierce faith; a faith that has nothing to do with belief, ideas, or ideology. This is a faith that leaves you with nothing to cling to and nowhere to hide. This faith strips you naked and leaves you exposed to the Truth: *alles iz Gott*, all is God.

33 □ Attaining True Joy

To attain true joy,
contemplate God
permeating all things.
Realize that this world
is nothing but divine glory
and that all things are empty
when seen from the perspective of God.[1]

God is the sole reality,
and wherever you look
it is God and God alone.[2]

Just as distinct rays of sunlight
are nothing but the sun,
so creation is nothing but God
and emptied of all self.

When you contemplate nonduality,
deeply and at length,
you are filled with uncontainable joy
and a faith so tremendous as to
realize your own oneness with God.[3]

(continued on page 107)

4   Kehot edition, p. 149.

5   Talmud, *Makkot* 24a.

6   Kehot edition, p. 151.

▤ The goal of the inbetweener is to realize the true nature of reality as the outpouring of divine creativity. *Tanya* offers many paths to this realization, hoping in this way to help people find a path that works for them. The path of the intellect is the path of contemplation. Remember that the intellect (*seichel*) has three faculties: intuitive wisdom (*Chochmah*), rational understanding (*Binah*), and integrative knowledge (*Da'at*). Let each of these faculties begin to see all things as God. Intuitively you know that nothing can survive in isolation, that all things are part of the singular system of life that is God. Engage this insight rationally. Look as hard as you wish to find something that is separate from its environment, other than the environment. The harder you look, the more you are convinced that your intuition is true: there is nothing but the One Thing. As intuition and reason align, your knowing is transformed. You are no longer a subject looking at the world as an object; you are the world looking at itself.

This realization releases a deep and transformative sense of wonder, which in turn releases an overwhelming joy. This joy permeates body, heart, mind, and soul, momentarily emptying all sense of self into the infinite oneness of pure spirit.

When the self returns, and it always returns, for the goal is not to empty the self but to have the self realize it is empty, a deep and abiding faith arises. It is a contentless faith without creed, a faith that allows you to live with humility and grace knowing that all is God.

This realization is the sole
purpose of your existence
and the purpose of all creation:
that the One should dwell as the many.[4]

This is the living faith,
as our Sages taught,
"The righteous will live by faith."[5, 6]

1 Talmud, *Shabbat* 88b. The Rabbis taught that the intensity of God's revelation was so great as to erase the sense of separate selfhood in all those present. They would "die" with each word and then return in the moment between words.

2 In 586 BCE and again in 70 CE.

3 *Halachah*, often rendered as "law," comes from the Hebrew *halach*, "to walk," and refers to the way Jews live by observing the 613 *mitzvot* (spiritual practices) of Judaism. Doing *mitzvot* is the way Jews walk in the world.

4 Kehot edition, p. 153.

5 *Tikkunei Zohar*, Introduction, 17a.

6 *Tzedakah*.

7 Talmud, *Bava Batra* 9a.

8 Kehot edition, p. 155.

≣ *Halachah*, the body of spiritual practices (*mitzvot*) that compose Jewish spiritual practice, is designed to awaken the self to its interdependence with all other selves without necessitating the emptying of self altogether. No *mitzvah* does this more powerfully than *tzedakah*, generosity toward the poor.

Tzedakah is not the same as charity. Charity, from the Latin *caritas*, "heart," links the act of giving to an a priori sense of caring. *Tzedakah*, from the Hebrew *tzedek*, "justice" requires only a sense of obligation to the welfare of others. The key is not to feel first and then act accordingly, but to act first and then see what feelings arise.

Because *tzedakah* is the right arm of God, the person who gives *tzedakah* becomes the right arm of God. The giving of *tzedakah* is not egoic; God is giving, you are merely the means. Knowing this awakens you to the realization that everything is the body of God, and this is why *tzedakah* is equal to all other *mitzvot*, because it awakens you to the unity toward which all *mitzvot* point.

34 □ Generosity

The revelation at Sinai
emptied the people of selfhood,
and "their souls departed with every word."[1]

To preserve the self,
God commanded the people
to build the Holy of Holies
in which God's presence would dwell,
and where divine unity would be revealed.

When the Temple was destroyed,
and with it the Holy of Holies,[2]
the Way[3] became God's dwelling place,
and spiritual practice became
a path to self-emptying.[4]

Chief among the spiritual practices is generosity,[5]
for "generosity is the right arm of God."[6]

The practice of generosity is equivalent
to all other spiritual practices.[7, 8]

[1] Deuteronomy 30:14.

[2] Kehot edition, p. 155.

[3] *Assiyah*.

[4] *Neshamah* and the *kelipat nogah*.

[5] *Neshamah*, your egoic intelligence.

[6] *Nefesh*, your physical intelligence.

[7] *Ruach*, your emotional intelligence.

[8] Selfless acts of loving-kindness.

[9] Kehot edition, pp. 157–159.

▤ *Assiyah*, the physical world of action, is the densest of all the worlds, and the one most in need of illumination. Just as a windowless room can only be illumined from within, so *Assiyah* must be illumined from within. You are the vehicle for that illumination, and you accomplish it by doing *maasim tovim*, selfless acts of loving-kindness.

In the world of action, only action matters. Feeling is not enough. Thinking is not enough. You must act. And when you act well, your actions illumine the world.

35 □ The Task of Self

"For the matter is very near to you,
in your mouth and in your heart,
that you may do it."[1, 2]

What is the meaning of "do it"?
Why does God manifest the physical world[3]
and clothe the ego in the shell of self?[4]

The self[5] is a holy flame.
The body[6] is the wick
keeping the self grounded
in this world.
The heart[7] is the oil that saturates the wick
and feeds the flame.
Acts of kindness[8] are the light
the self brings to the world.
This is the "it" you are commanded to do.[9]

[1] *Midrash Tanchuma, Naso* 7:1.

[2] Exodus 33:20. Seeing God directly annihilates the self completely.

[3] *Hishtalshelut,* "chain," refers to the flowing of God's energy from world to world—from *Adam Kadmon* to *Assiyah,* the world of pure spirit to the world of pure matter.

36 □ No High or Low in God

Our Sages taught
that the world was created
as a lower dwelling place for God.[1]
Yet, do not imagine there is
a literal "higher" and "lower" in God,
for God pervades all reality equally.

"Higher" and "lower" apply only
to your way of perceiving,
as it is written,
"No one can see Me and live."[2]
To prevent this direct seeing,
God veils light in a chain of forms,[3]
each link more dense than the one before
and culminating in our physical world.

(continued on page 115)

4 | Zephaniah 2:15.

5 | Kehot edition, p. 163.

▤ | The Alter Rebbe imagines God's unfolding as a chain, with each link being a different world and each world containing its own distinct intelligence, its own way of perceiving and knowing. God's nonduality (*shlemut*) necessitates the emanation of everything and its opposite, the world of pure Godhead balanced by the world of pure selfhood. The task of the inbetweener is to realize that all five worlds are equally God.

The challenge the inbetweener faces is the preoccupation of *Neshamah* with the "lower" worlds of *Assiyah, Yetzirah*, and *Beriah* (physical, emotional, and egoic). Focusing on the self, *Neshamah* falls into the darkness of *kelipat nogah* (egoic shell), imagining that it is other than and isolated from all beings and God, saying, "There is nothing else besides me."

The work of the inbetweener is to awaken *Neshamah*'s intellect, especially its capacity for *Chochmah*, wisdom, and thereby open it to the "higher" worlds and ways of knowing that reveal first the interconnectedness of all things in God (the world of *Atzilut* and *Chayyah* intelligences) and then the nonduality of God as all things (the world of *Adam Kadmon* and *Yechidah* intelligences).

With the awakening of *Yechidah*, the sense of separate self ends completely, hence, "No one can see Me and live." But this is not the end of the matter. For the inbetweener, it isn't about annihilating the self forever, but about bringing about the rebirth of the self in a more integrative whole. So the inbetweener returns to the dark and once again strives to kindle more light.

So concealed is the light of God in our world,
that we imagine ourselves as gods, saying,
"I am, and there is nothing else besides me."[4]

The purpose of God's chain of emanation is
to provide our world,
the darkest and most dense world,
the world of shells and otherness,
with the opportunity
to realize light in the midst of darkness
and thereby delight God,
who values light and darkness
even more than light alone.[5]

1 The "dead" are those living people closed to the reality of God in and as all reality.

2 The direct way to revive the "dead" is to crack the shells (*kelipot*) that separate them from the whole. The doing of *mitzvot* (spiritual practices) is designed to shatter that shell of otherness and self-isolation.

3 Kehot edition, p. 167.

4 This is true for the person doing a *mitzvah*, for anything used in the doing of a *mitzvah*, and for anyone who receives the benefit of a *mitzvah*.

5 The task of the inbetweener is not to transcend the physical world, but to live in it as a beacon of light illuminating the Presence of God that is the essence of all things.

6 *Mitzvah stam*.

7 Kehot edition, p. 175.

8 Talmud, *Bava Batra* 10a. *Tzedakah* involves money earned and money given away. Earning money requires your full engagement in the physical world: body, heart, and mind. Doing so justly, and with the intent of helping both self and others, engages the soul as well, hallowing everything involved in earning one's livelihood. Giving money away to the poor requires that you surrender ownership of what you have earned and in so doing erases the shell of separation between the one who gives and those who receive. The engagement of body, heart, mind, and soul, coupled with the breaking of the shells of separation, brings us to the brink of full God-realization with its complete redemption.

9 Kehot edition, p. 177.

37 □ Illuminating the World

The messianic perfection
and the resurrection of the dead,
which are the revelation of the Infinite
in the heart of the finite,[1]
depend entirely upon you
and your spiritual practice.[2, 3]

When physically engaged in spiritual practice,
the shells of separation are made transparent,
and the light of God
illumines the darkness of self.[4]

You are not here
to elevate the spiritual,
but to illumine the material.
Illumination happens when you
eat, drink, and do all you do
in a state of holiness.[5]

The greatest illumination
comes through generosity,
which is called the quintessential practice.[6, 7]

Generosity is giving from the fruits of your labor
and requires all of your energy.
Your entire body gives and uplifts it.
This is why generosity hastens redemption.[8, 9]

1 Talmud, *Berachot* 20b.

2 Kehot edition, p. 179.

3 The *Sh'ma* (the Hearing) is the central affirmation of Judaism: "Hear, O Israel, *YHVH* is our God, *YHVH* is One" (Deuteronomy 6:4). The *Sh'ma* is recited at least twice daily and is to be the final words you utter upon death.

4 The purpose of prayer is to rouse you to action. If your prayer remains only in your mind, it has no impact on your actions. But if prayer is said aloud, the body is engaged and motivated to act.

5 *Kavanah*, concentration of the mind with the intention of illuminating God in all dimensions.

6 *Shnei Luchot HaBrit* 1:249b.

7 Kehot edition, p. 181.

8 Kehot edition, pp. 183–185.

≣ Rabbi Schneur Zalman is concerned lest the inbetweener become preoccupied with self-transcendence and neglect the physical dimensions of life. It is all too easy to place "spiritual" in opposition to "material" and then to neglect the latter in favor of the former. *Tanya* is clear: complete awakening happens in and through all five worlds. The true work of the spiritual person is to infuse the material world with spiritual light and thus illumine the Divine in, with, and as all reality. There is no distinction between matter and spirit in God. There is only God.

Thus, contemplative practices must include the body rather than exclude it. Even when reciting the *Sh'ma*, the affirmation of God's non-duality, the body must be engaged, at least through the act of speech. But the words must not be empty. On the contrary, they must be infused with *kavanah*, an intense focus of the intellect (*seichel*) that uses the act of prayer as a means for engaging the body, heart, mind, and soul in illuminating all worlds.

38 □ The Necessity of Intent

Thought alone is incapable
of bringing about redemption.
Prayer without speech is unacceptable.[1, 2]

This is true even of the *Sh'ma*,[3]
which must be articulated out loud.
All prayers or blessings must be spoken aloud,
for if the body is not engaged,
the material world cannot be healed.[4]

Yet speech alone is incapable
of bringing about redemption.
While prayer without concentration[5]
fulfills the obligation to pray,
prayer without concentration
is like a body without breath.[6, 7]

Prayer is not superior to action,
nor is action superior to prayer.
Both are desired by God.[8]

1 Kehot edition, p. 193.

2 Kehot edition, p. 195.

3 *Lishmah*, "for its own sake," is a deed done without any ulterior motive.

4 The unification of body, heart, mind, soul, and spirit in the realization that God is all.

5 You have more control over your thoughts than your feelings, so the Alter Rebbe is not insisting you need arouse both equally.

6 Love supports both lover and beloved, while awe and wonder surrender the lover to the Beloved, God.

39 □ Acting without Ulterior Motive

Know without doubt
that the purpose of spiritual practice
is the realization of God.

Such practices release your capacity
for self-effacing wonder and love,
a capacity latent in every mind and heart.[1]

It is not sufficient
to arouse one or the other:
both heart and mind must be engaged,
and this requires intense concentration.[2]

Spiritual practices done from habit or rote
are without effect;
only service for its own sake[3] has the capacity
to lift you toward unification,[4]
and such practice is impossible without
love in your mind
and at least a little in your heart.[5]
Nor is love alone enough,
for awe and wonder are also needed.[6]

(continued on page 123)

[7] The Alter Rebbe continually reaches out to even the least spiritually inclined person. No one should despair of realizing God. If you act from rote, eventually you will desire more from your actions and in this way be inspired to cultivate concentration (*kavanah*).

[8] Second Samuel 14:14.

[9] Kehot edition, p. 197.

[≣] Awe and wonder empty the self (*Neshamah*) into God in a moment of ecstatic bliss. For a timeless moment the self is erased in the greater unity of God. When the moment passes, God's love pours back into the self, and *Neshamah* returns transformed. Having tasted the greater unity of which it is a part, *Neshamah* no longer clings to its fragmented sense of self, but allows the *kelipat nogah* (egoic shell) to become transparent to the light of God flowing through all worlds. No longer alienated from the Whole, you feel an intense love for the Whole. Acting *lishmah*, engaging in spiritual practices without thought of reward, triggers the emptying of self and the inpouring of God.

Not everyone can act *lishmah*, but that should not trouble you. The realization that *lishmah* is absent kindles the desire for *lishmah* that will eventually lead to *lishmah*. This is why "no one banished from God remains banished" (2 Samuel 14:14). As soon as you know you are banished from God, you are aware of God and hence no longer banished at all.

Yet even if you act selfishly,
even if you act from habit and rote,
there is still hope.[7]
For those who act selfishly
will eventually realize their mistake
and act selflessly,
as it is written,
"No one banished from God remains banished."[8, 9]

1 *Tikkunei Zohar, Tikkun* 57, p. 91b.

2 Isaiah 45:15. God is hidden and not absent. Do not imagine God is hidden inside the physical, for that would imply that God does not fill all dimensions. No, God is hidden as the physical. It is our insistence that God cannot be a thing that prevents us from seeing God manifest as all things.

3 Kehot edition, p. 199.

40 □ Revealing the Hidden God

Although God and Torah are one—
for Torah is God's will and
there is no division between will
and the One who wills it—
and despite the fact that God fills all worlds equally,
there are still differences among worlds.

The higher the world, the fewer the veils;
the fewer the veils, the more intense the light.
The material world is the lowest and most veiled,
so veiled that light appears solid
and the self appears isolated and alone.

And while "no place is devoid of God,"[1]
in our world God is called "a hidden God."[2, 3]

(continued on page 127)

4   Isaiah 40:5. The glory of God will be revealed to all flesh through all flesh. In other words, the body has to be engaged along with the heart, mind, and soul in the realization of God and godliness. When this level of engagement is achieved, you will see all shells and dimensions as manifestations of the One Reality.

5   Kehot edition, p. 205.

≣   From God's perspective there is only God. The five worlds or dimensions—*Assiyah, Yetzirah, Beriah, Atzilut,* and *Adam Kadmon*—are different frequencies of God's infinite light and not other than that light. The intelligence of each world—*Nefesh, Ruach, Neshamah, Chayyah,* and *Yechidah,* respectively—is the instrument by which specific frequencies can be perceived. There are two reasons why God remains hidden from us: first, because we fail to use all five faculties; and second, because we insist that the frequencies of God revealed to *Nefesh, Ruach, Neshamah* (the intelligences of body, heart, and mind) are not in fact God. This explains the seeming contradictory teachings that "no place is devoid of God" (*Tikkunei Zohar, Tikkun* 57, p. 91b) and God is "a hidden God" (Isaiah 45:15). While every place is filled with God, only those attuned to the right frequencies can see this. As for the rest, God is hidden.

The study of Torah
reveals the hidden God,
for, again, God and Torah are one.
But this is true only
when Torah is spoken aloud
and with concentration,
for then body, heart, and mind
are filled with divine understanding
and the shell of self is emptied
into the unity of God, as it is written,
"The glory of God will be revealed
for all flesh to behold."[4, 5]

[1] Jeremiah 23:24.

[2] Talmud, *Sanhedrin* 4:5.

[3] Kehot edition, p. 205.

[4] Love rests *on* your heart rather than in your heart. Love surrounds your heart. You must open your heart to allow love to permeate it. You open your heart when you remember your total dependence on creation and are overwhelmed with gratitude and humility.

41 □ Love and Awe

Love and awe are like two wings of a bird.
Just as a bird cannot fly with only one wing,
so you cannot rise to the higher worlds
with only one wing.

To arouse awe you must, at the very least,
contemplate the boundless spaciousness of God
which encompasses all dimensions,
as it is written,
"Do I not fill heaven and earth?"[1]

When such awe is aroused,
you realize that the entire
universe conspires to
bring you into being, saying,
"For my sake was the world created."[2, 3]

Meditate on this to the best of your ability,
and realize your obligation to the world,
recalling this obligation prior to any act.

Love, too, must be cultivated,
and doing so is a bit easier,
for love already rests on[4] your heart.
All you need do is remember it.

(continued on page 131)

5 | Talmud, *Berachot* 49b.

6 | Kehot edition, p. 211.

≣ | Awe is the experience of God's presence in all the worlds and in all their manifestations. When you see God in everything as everything, you are then enveloped in *ahavah rabbah,* the infinite love *of* God that fills you with an infinite love *for* God and all creation.

This is what Hillel (70 BCE–10 CE), one of the greatest of the ancient Rabbis, means when he says, "Do not separate yourself from the community" (Talmud, *Berachot* 49b). The community is the entirety of reality, manifest and unmanifest. Separating from the community happens when the shell of separate self (*kelipat nogah*) blinds you to the Presence of God and leaves you with the mistaken notion that seeing God requires you to abandon the material world and the physical pleasures it offers. Spiritual practice is not escaping from one world to another, but the realization that all worlds are God.

As love and awe uplift you to God,
Remember the words of Hillel,
"Do not separate yourself from the community."[5]
Do not abandon the lower for the higher,
but reveal them all as God.[6]

[1] Jeremiah 31:34.

[2] Kehot edition, p. 217.

[3] Talmud, *Megillah* 6b. Only those who make a concerted effort are to be believed.

[4] Kehot edition, pp. 220–221.

[5] Actions that abuse the body, arouse the body for its own sake, or exploit the bodies of others.

42 □ Your Inner "Moses"

Every person contains a
capacity called "Moses"
that allows them to bring
the knowledge of God into the community.

Some contain more "Moses" than others,
and these can teach people to know God.
They will remain among us
until the messianic era, as it is written,
"And they shall teach no more …
for all shall know Me."[1, 2]

But such knowing is only in the mind,
and your body, too, must
feel God's presence.
This no one can teach you.
Only your own effort can achieve this.
Hence, "If a person says,
'I have labored and found,' believe him."[3, 4]

To achieve this physical knowing
you must first control your drives
and refrain from actions that
obscure the light of God.[5]

(continued on page 135)

| 6 | *Emunah* is conventionally understood as "faith," but the Alter Rebbe is emphasizing the necessity of practice.

| 7 | Kehot edition, p. 225.

[≣] God provides us with teachers of God-realization. They "know the God of your father, and serve Him with a whole heart and a longing soul" (1 Chronicles 28:9). Their task is to help you know God and not to serve themselves in any way. In fact, the role of the spiritual teacher is self-eliminating: "And they shall teach no more every man his neighbor, and every man his brother, saying, 'Know YHVH,' for all shall know Me" (Jeremiah 31:34). The aim of a spiritual teacher is to make teaching unnecessary and knowing universal.

Yet even with the help of teachers, spirituality is work (*avodah*). And like all work, it can be tedious and exhausting. This is why we are taught to seek God as if seeking a hidden treasure (Proverbs 2:4–5). Just as you would not give up because the digging is hard work, so do not abandon your practice because contemplation is hard. This is the meaning of the word *emunah*, "faith." You have faith not in this or that idea or creed, but faith in the process, so you discipline yourself to stick with it, to keep digging. The essential thing is to train and habituate your mind continuously so that it always knows, sees, and hears the physical world as a manifestation of God.

Second, you must arouse the imagination,
and feel your body afloat in the Infinite.
spaciousness of God.
This must be done for long periods of time,
though how long differs with each person.

The essential thing is to train
both heart and mind to see
all things as God.
This is implicit in the word "faith,"[6]
which we should understand to mean training.[7]

1 The Hebrew word here is *yirah*, which means both "awe" and "fear."

2 *Yirah tata'ah*, "lower awe."

3 Psalm 34:15.

4 *Pirke Avot* 3:17a. Fear precedes wisdom because it causes the self to restrain itself, and in this moment of restraint lies the possibility of realizing the interconnectedness of self and other that wisdom contains.

5 *Yirah ila'ah*, "higher awe."

6 *Pirke Avot* 3:17b. Wisdom precedes wonder because it reveals the interdependence of all things in God and allows for the possibility of realizing the nonduality of all things as God.

7 Kehot edition, p. 227.

8 *Ahavat olam*, "worldly [*olam*] love [*ahavah*]," reflects the longings of *Nefesh*, *Ruach*, and *Neshamah*: *Nefesh* (body) longs for pleasure, *Ruach* (heart) longs for companionship, and *Neshamah* (mind) longs for immortality.

9 *Ahavah rabbah*, "unending [*rabbah*] love," reflects the longings of *Chayyah* and *Yechidah*: *Chayyah* (soul) longs for unity with all things in God, and *Yechidah* (spirit) longs for the nonduality of all things as God.

10 Kehot edition, p. 229.

≣ Worldly love (*ahavat olam*) is never completely satisfying because it depends on an other who is both ever-changing and impermanent. In time the suffering caused by worldly love leads to a desire for something more and kindles the greater love (*ahavah rabbah*). At this point, you seek out a spiritual teacher and take the first steps from self-focused fear and longing to selfless awe and love.

43 ☐ Two Types of Awe

There are two levels of awe,[1] one lower and one higher.
The lower awe[2] is experienced as fear,
particularly a fear of harming others.
This fear fills you with the desire to
"turn from evil and do good."[3]
About this type of awe our Sages said,
"If there is no fear, there is no wisdom."[4]

The higher awe[5] is experienced as wonder
so intense that it overwhelms the self with the glory of God.
Of this awe our Sages said,
"If there is no wisdom, there is no wonder."[6, 7]

Just as there are two grades of awe,
so are there two grades of love, one lower and one higher.
The lesser love is a longing for connections in the world.[8]
The greater love is realization of one's connection with God.[9, 10]

[1] Isaiah 26:9. Grammatically, "You" refers to "soul," but for the Alter Rebbe, God and soul are one. Hence he takes "You" to refer to God.

[2] The *Zohar*, the thirteenth-century Book of Splendor, is the central text of Kabbalah.

[3] *Zohar* 3:67a.

[4] Kehot edition, pp. 231–233.

[5] *Zohar* 3:281a.

[6] Malachi 2:10.

[7] Deuteronomy 30:11.

[8] Kehot edition, p. 233.

44 □ Higher Grades of Love

There is a third grade of love,
higher still, that all people share.
This love is hinted at in the verse
"My soul, I desire You at night."[1]
About this the *Zohar*[2] says,
"Since You, God, are my true nature and life,
I desire You with the intensity of the dying
who yet desperately cling to life."[3, 4]

There is a fourth grade of love,
higher still, that also resides in everyone.
This love is "like a child whose love
for her parents surpasses her love of self
and who acts for their sake alone."[5]

Since we all have "one Father,"[6]
we all have this love hidden deep within.
Anyone can access this love;
it is "not beyond reach, nor is it far off,
but it is very close to you, in your mouth and heart."[7, 8]

All four kinds of love should be cultivated.
This is the reason you were created.

(*continued on page 141*)

9 Talmud, *Kiddushin* 40a.

10 Kehot edition, p. 235.

≡ No one is excluded from spiritual awakening. While not everyone is ready for the practice of self-emptying awe or open to the guidance of a spiritual teacher, everyone has the innate capacity to be transformed through love.

How is this done? Through the power of loving speech. Speak in such a manner that promotes harmony rather than discord, peace rather than conflict. Use your words to recognize the unity embracing all diversity. Since words are linked to thoughts, and both are linked to deeds (together forming the Three Garments of the intellect), habituating your speech to love arouses both mind and heart to love, and together they will align your actions with love as well. You may not be able to directly control your thoughts and feelings, and your actions may be driven by habits too deep to dispel, but the words that come out of your mouth, these are controllable. Begin with what is "in your mouth" to arouse what is in your heart and mind, and in time your actions will be in tune with God and godliness.

How is such love released?
Speak to one another in a manner
that arouses your heart and mind to yearn for God,
for it is written,
"A good thought is joined by God to a deed."[9, 10]

[1] Kehot edition, p. 237.

[2] *Ayn Sof*, the Infinite Godhead, includes even the thickest shell of self and separation, for even these are part of God's infinite unfolding.

[3] We feel exiled from the *Shechinah*, God's Immanence, when we forget our true nature as manifestations of God.

[4] When you realize your attachment to self is preventing you from realizing the unity of the transcendent and the immanent aspects of God, you will desire that union and work to end your attachment.

[5] Isaiah 55:7.

[6] Genesis 29:11.

[7] *Yichud elyon*, literally the "highest unity," that is, nonduality.

45 □ Compassion for God

There is another path open to everyone,
and that is cultivating compassion for God.[1]

The blessed Endless One[2] permeates all reality,
yet the forms it takes forget their true nature
and fall prey to the delusion of alienation.
This is called the Exile of the *Shechinah*.[3]

When you realize you are the cause of this Exile,[4]
you will feel compassion for God, as it is written,
"And let him return to God and have mercy upon him."[5]

This is also the meaning of the verse
"And Jacob kissed Rachel
and lifted up his voice and wept."[6]
Jacob represents the quality of mercy,
and Rachel the source of all life.
Jacob felt such love for Rachel
that he lifted his voice and strengthened his compassion,
and in his love united both himself and Rachel
in the highest unity.[7]

(continued on page 145)

8 Song of Songs 1:2.

9 *Halachah,* the way of the *mitzvot.*

10 *Tzedakah* and *chesed.*

11 Kehot edition, p. 239.

≣ As your words open you to deeper and deeper expressions of love, you will come to see the suffering that arises from the insistence on a separate and independent self. Your entire being will yearn to bring peace and harmony to the world by revealing the true nature of all as God. You will have compassion for God, who, being all things, suffers as all things, and you will long to end this suffering by revealing the truth of *yichud elyon,* the absolute unity of all things in, with, and as God.

The means for this revelation is the holy path of *mitzvot,* those actions designed to bridge the imagined gap between self, other, and God. Among the *mitzvot,* the two that do this most profoundly are generosity (*tzedakah*) and compassion (*chesed*). *Tzedakah,* acting generously and promoting economic justice, frees you from a self-centered sense of ownership built on a the notion of scarcity and awakens you to the greater truth that life's abundance comes to us not to horde but to share. In this sharing, giver and receiver become one and know the One.

The same is true of *chesed,* selfless acts of kindness, *maasim tovim,* that awaken us to our true purpose: loving our neighbor as our self. As this love fills us, we realize that our neighbor is our self, that we are both part of a single system of life that is the outpouring of God.

This unity is called the "Level of Kisses,"
where breath meets breath, as it is written,
"Let Him kiss me with the kisses of His mouth."[8]

How is this achieved in the world?
Through the way of spiritual practice,[9]
especially the practice of generosity and kindness.[10, 11]

1 Proverbs 27:19.

2 Kehot edition, p. 241.

3 *Mitzrayim*, "Egypt," is a pun meaning "narrow places." The Exodus from Egypt is an ongoing liberation from all the narrow places in which you are enslaved.

4 Exodus 3:8; the "descent" of God is the manifestation of the Infinite as the finite. Salvation is the realization of the Infinite by the finite.

5 Kehot edition, p. 243.

6 The Alter Rebbe is paraphrasing the theme of the Song of Songs, thought to be authored by King Solomon.

7 Kehot edition, p. 245.

≣ The friendship the Alter Rebbe is proposing is that intimate friendship between bridegroom and bride. This is called *kiddushin*, "betrothal." When you do a *mitzvah*, it is often prefaced by a blessing containing the word *kid'shanu*, conventionally translated as "God has sanctified us." The deeper meaning is that through the self-emptying *mitzvot* you are about to perform, you are betrothed to God, taken up in the loving embrace of bridegroom and bride.

Tanya is saying that just as friends act lovingly toward one another, and lovers all the more so, when you realize you are loved by God, you will return that love, not in some mystical abstract manner, but by actively loving others through the performance of *mitzvot*, especially generosity (*tzedakah*) and compassion (*chesed*).

46 □ Way of Friendship

There is yet another direct way to God,
that is near to you.
This is the way of friendship
revealed in the verse
"As water mirrors face to face,
so the heart of one mirrors the heart of another."[1, 2]

As love between friends
circles from one to the other
in an endless round,
so too the love of God.

God's love lifts you out of narrowness[3]
not through any intermediary
but by Himself, alone, as it is written,
"And I descended to save him."[4]
God's love lifts us to true intimacy
and unity with God.[5]

You reflect this love back to God
through spiritual practice.
This is what Solomon calls
the union of bridegroom and bride.[6, 7]

1 *Mitzrayim*; *Mishnah Pesachim* 10:5.

2 *Ayn Sof*, the Absolute Godhead.

3 Genesis 12:9.

4 Kehot edition, p. 247.

47 □ Release from Bondage

"In every generation and every day
you are obligated to regard yourself
as if you had that day come out of narrowness."[1]

This refers to your release
from the illusions of separateness
and your absorption into
the light of the blessed Endless One.[2]

Abraham achieved release
through his own effort,
advancing in holiness by degrees, as it is written,
"And Abram journeyed, going on and on."[3, 4]

This is fine for Abraham,
but you need not advance
through your own effort,
for God gifts you with release through Torah.
To understand Torah is to
realize your oneness with God,
and in this way to be released from narrowness.

(continued on page 151)

5 *Zohar* 2:162b.

6 Kehot edition, p. 249.

≣ "In every generation"—the Alter Rebbe adds "and every day"—
"we are obligated to regard ourselves as if we had that day come out
of *Mitzrayim*" (*Mishnah Pesachim* 10:5). *Mitzrayim*, "Egypt," refers
not simply to the historical land of the Pharaohs, but is also a Hebrew
pun on the word *tzar'im*, which means "narrow places." Egypt represents those places in which you find yourself enslaved to false gods,
ideas, harmful emotions, and hurtful behavior. Most systems of spiritual
growth take the Abrahamic approach, encouraging you to free yourself
from *Mitzrayim* step-by-step. But the Alter Rebbe is offering a different view: you are already free; you just don't realize it.

Today, this very moment, you are one with God. Today, this very
moment, you can achieve *da'at devekut*, the realization of this oneness. There is nothing you have to do except to stop insisting that
things are other than they are.

You are like a person dying of thirst who sits next to a tall glass of
cool, fresh water. So convinced are you that there is no water, you completely ignore the reality right in front of you. You don't have to ask
for water or fetch it yourself. All you have to do is stop ignoring the
water that is offered, and drink. And when you do drink, your thirst is
gone immediately.

It is the same with God's oneness. As soon as you realize the Presence of God in and as all things, including yourself, your sense of separation and the anxiety it produces are gone. This is what *Tanya* calls
"spirit evoking spirit," for you realize you are God calling to God.

When your desire for unity
overwhelms your desire for separation,
you are immediately absorbed in God,
for "spirit evokes spirit."[5]

This absorption is your coming out of narrowness.[6]

1 *Tzimtzum*, "contraction." The original understanding of *tzimtzum* involves the literal contraction of God from the center to the periphery, allowing space for creation. The Alter Rebbe understands *tzimtzum* as a progressive veiling of God's light to allow for the appearance of a separate reality.

2 *Sovev* (encompassing) *kol almin* (all worlds) is the Infinite embracing the finite. It is coupled with *memale kol almin*, the divine energy that permeates and animates all worlds. *Sovev kol almin* is the source of all reality; *memale kol almin* is its substance. And, of course, both are God.

3 Kehot edition, pp. 249–251.

4 Isaiah 6:3. The Alter Rebbe takes this to refer to *sovev kol almin*.

5 *Memale kol almin*.

6 Jeremiah 23:24. The Alter Rebbe takes this to refer to *memale kol almin*.

7 Isaiah 55:8.

8 Kehot edition, p. 253.

≣ When you contemplate infinity, the faculty of *Chochmah*, intuitive wisdom, reveals to you the all-pervasive nature of God. *Chochmah* floods *Binah*, rational understanding, and you realize that *Neshamah*, your sense of finite self, is a part of the infinite creativity of God. At that moment *Neshamah* is totally emptied into God. Anything short of this total extinction of *Neshamah* is not yet complete awakening.

Neshamah cannot will its own extinction. On the contrary, the very purpose of *Neshamah* is to avoid just such a thing. Thus, there is no concrete *mitzvah* for self-emptying. Rather, it is a natural by-product of the deliberate contemplation of God's vastness.

The emptying of self into God is like a wave returning to the ocean, and just as the ocean continues to wave, your sense of self returns, but transformed. Where prior to emptying you insisted you were other than God, upon returning you realize you are a unique manifestation of God. Now *Neshamah*'s task is to honor that uniqueness without mistaking it for otherness.

48 □ The Finite and the Infinite

Contemplating the spaciousness of the Endless One,
you come to realize God's infinity.

Realizing God's infinity
you awake to the finite as part of the Infinite.
The means by which the Infinite
becomes the finite is called contraction.[1]

The finite in no way constricts the Infinite,
for the Infinite encompasses all worlds.[2, 3]

The Infinite embraces the finite, as it is written,
"The whole world is full of His glory,"[4]
The Infinite permeates all worlds,[5]
as it is written,
"Do I not fill heaven and earth?"[6]

Constriction applies to your thoughts
and not to God.
Your thoughts maintain your separate self,
but, as it is written,
"My thoughts are not your thoughts."[7]
While you see yourself as apart from God,
God sees you as a part of God.[8]

1 The infinity of God necessitates infinite gradations of God.

2 *Beriah, Yetzirah,* and *Assiyah.*

3 Talmud, *Bava Metzia* 84a. Just as the blackness of space highlights the shining of the stars, so the physicality of the world highlights the shining of the spirit.

4 Kehot edition, pp. 255–257.

5 Isaiah 40:5. Just as human love impels the physical lover toward the beloved, so divine love impels the material world toward the realization of its divine source and essence.

6 Kehot edition, p. 261.

☰ God's contraction goes with God's expansion the way inhalation goes with exhalation, and both are necessary expressions of God's nonduality.

The material worlds appear dark, dense, solid, and other, hence they are called *sitra achra*, the other side of God's unity. This darkness allows the light of God's unity to shine and in this way to be known throughout the *sitra achra*.

It is not enough to know this intellectually. It must permeate body, heart, and mind and cultivate actions that honor and hallow all five dimensions of reality. This is how the Alter Rebbe understands "And the glory of God shall be revealed, and all flesh shall see it" (Isaiah 40:5). The glory of God, the infinity of God's light shining as all worlds, is perceived even in the most dense world of physical matter.

You hallow *Assiyah*, the world of doing, by doing justly. You hallow *Yetzirah*, the world of feeling, by loving mercy. You hallow *Beriah*, the world of thinking, by walking humbly with God. You hallow *Atzilut*, the world of relating, by "loving your neighbor as your self," knowing all beings to be part of your self. And you hallow *Adam Kadmon*, the world of being, by loving God with all your heart, with all your mind, and with all you have and are, and in this way making clear the One is all.

49 □ The Purpose of Creation

While the levels of contraction
are too many to count,[1]
we focus on three:
the world of thinking, the world of feeling, and the world of
    doing.[2]

Thinking, feeling, and doing
are essential to the material world,
whose purpose is to provide darkness
in which light can shine.
Hence the purpose of descent
is in fact ascent,
for "love impels the flesh."[3, 4]

It is not enough to know this,
you must also act upon it,
as it is written,
"And the glory of God shall be revealed,
and all flesh shall see it."[5]

This is why God contracted
and became the worlds,
to draw the Infinite into the finite
that the finite might know the Infinite.[6]

1 *Kesef hakodashim*, from 2 Kings 12:5, "All silver [*kesef*] donated for holy purposes [*kadoshim*] is to be brought to the house of *YHVH*."

2 Genesis 31:3. The Alter Rebbe is playing with the words *kesef*, "silver," and *kasaf*, "yearning." This holy silver is your innate yearning to melt into the infinite spaciousness of God, as a lover yearns to melt into the arms of the beloved.

3 This is a reference to Song of Songs 2:5.

4 *Klot hanefesh* from Psalm 84:3, the annihilation of the separate self in the infinite spaciousness of God.

5 Kehot edition, p. 263.

6 *Ratzo*, "hastening," and *shov*, "returning."

7 *Tikkunei Zohar*, Introduction, 7a. When you feel the pull of Infinity, surrender to it, and do not fear it.

50 □ Run and Return

All the levels of love
spoken of so far
are called "holy silver,"[1]
as in the words
"You greatly yearned for your father's house."[2]

But there is another level of love
that exceeds these as gold exceeds silver.
This love is like glowing coals of fire
and is kindled through meditation
on the infinite spaciousness of God
and the complete emptying of all things
into absolute nothing that such meditation generates.

In this emptying,
the flame desires to separate from the coals,
its yearning is so great that it is lovesick,[3]
and this great yearning brings about its own demise.[4, 5]

This level of love generates hastening and returning,[6]
as it is written,
"If your heart hastens, return to One."[7]

(continued on page 159)

8 *Pirke Avot* 4:22. Just as the tide ebbs and flows, so you will be emptied into God and then returned to the world transformed.

9 *Zohar* 2:135a.

10 Kehot edition, p. 265.

≋ You are made to love God, and through that love to be emptied of self and selfishness and then returned to the world transformed. The Alter Rebbe is playing with the text "Come, my beloved, to meet the bride" (*Lecha Dodi,* Shabbat liturgy). The Hebrew word for "brides" is *kallot,* which Rabbi Schneur Zalman links with *klot,* "annihilation." When the bride is embraced in the beloved, she loses herself in his embrace. The bride is you; the beloved is the Infinite Godhead (*Ayn Sof*).

Once lost in the arms of the Beloved, you discover that Infinity includes finity, that the *sitra achra* is the other side of God, the side of the many who are all manifestations of the One. At that moment you return to the other side with a love so great as to burn away the illusion of separateness and help you discover your true essence as a manifestation of God.

"If your heart hastens"
is the moment of self-emptying
from which you must
return to the world,
for "despite yourself you must live."[8]

Your task is not to escape this world
but to reveal it as a manifestation of God,
as it is written,
"That there be One in one."[9, 10]

[1] *Shechinah* is the felt Presence of God.

[2] Isaiah 6:3.

[3] Job 19:26.

[4] Kehot edition, p. 265.

[5] Kehot edition, p. 269.

[≡] Each of the five worlds has its own intelligence or way of knowing, and each intelligence has its own way of knowing God. *Assiyah/Nefesh* experiences God as natural law; *Yetzirah/Ruach* as primal love and fear; *Beriah/Neshamah* as an idea or ideal; *Atzilut/Chayyah* as the many; and *Adam Kadmon/Yechidah* as the Only One. Of the five, only *Neshamah*'s way of knowing makes of God an other and situates that Other in time and space. This situated God is *Shechinah*.

The Alter Rebbe's concern here is that you see through the limitations of *Neshamah* and not imagine that *Shechinah* is somewhere rather than everywhere, and sometime rather than right now. This removal of *Neshamah*'s delusions is the work of the inbetweener.

51 □ The Dwelling of God

How shall we understand the phrase
"the *Shechinah* dwells"?[1]
It cannot be that God
dwells in one place and not another,
for "the whole world is full of His glory."[2]

To understand "the *Shechinah* dwells"
you must understand the text
"And from my flesh I see God."[3, 4]

The flesh perceives everything
in terms of space and time,
hence the body's perception
of God dwelling
in space and time.

In this way we imagine consciousness
dwelling in the brain
when in fact it pervades the entire body.

Just as consciousness pervades the body,
so the Endless One fills all the worlds.
Just as consciousness is said
to dwell in the brain,
so God is said to dwell in the world.[5]

1 │ Just as the vitality of the sun is its rays of light, so the vitality of God is the continual rising and falling of *Yesh* and *Ayn*, form and emptiness.

2 │ *Chochmah, Binah,* and *Da'at*.

3 │ Through the contemplative study of Torah, you discover the inner meaning of the practices, informing your actions with intention (*kavanah*) and hence revealing the unity of all worlds in God.

4 │ *Matrunita*, Aramaic for "Queen." Where the King is often hidden and austere, the Queen embraces her people and is found among them, offering comfort and love. God as King is the sun consuming all in its fiery core. God as Queen is the sunlight that makes life and living possible.

5 │ Just as the rays of the sun take the sun to the outermost reaches of space, so the Divine Mother takes the power of God into the furthest reaches of the *sitra achra*, the other side.

6 │ Exodus 25:8. If the sun dwelt in our midst, we would be consumed in deadly flame. If sunlight did not dwell in our midst, we would be consumed by deadly ice. God's nature, Father and Mother, King and Queen, the transcendent *YHVH* and the immanent *Shechinah*, is perfectly suited for life in all dimensions.

7 │ Kehot edition, p. 271.

8 │ The purpose of Torah and *mitzvot*, instruction and practice, is to provide us with a way of living that softens the intensity of God's light in order to bring life-giving light to self and other.

9 │ Kehot edition, p. 273.

▤ The Alter Rebbe is not interested in the annihilation of this world by plunging it into the center of the sun, but in the hallowing of this world by bathing it in life-giving light. This is done through the study of Torah and the practice of *mitzvot*. Torah, read properly, reveals the reality of God in, with, and as all reality. *Mitzvot*, done properly, translates this revelation into acts of justice and compassion.

52 □ Perceiving the One

The vitality of God[1]
manifests as divine will,
intuitive wisdom, rational understanding,
and integrative knowledge[2]
and is clothed in Torah and spiritual practice.[3]

This vitality is called Queen[4]
and the outermost Mother[5]
and the *Shechinah*, from the verse
"And I will dwell among them."[6, 7]

Just as sunlight
makes it possible for us
to perceive the sun,
so *Shechinah* as Torah and spiritual practice
makes it possible for us to perceive the One.[8, 9]

1 | Exodus 32:16.

2 | Kehot edition, p. 277.

3 | Talmud, *Yoma*, 9b; *Berachot* 8a.

4 | Talmud, *Berachot* 6a.

5 | *Zohar* 3:187a, chapter 35.

6 | Kehot edition, p. 279.

7 | Deuteronomy 4:24.

8 | Kehot edition, p. 281.

When you contemplate and meditate on the words of Torah, the *Shechinah*, the Presence of God, rests upon your head, but it is still not embodied in your actions. To embody the *Shechinah* requires engagement with spiritual practice. By means of such practice you begin to illumine the darkness of the other side (*sitra achra*), cracking the shells of self and selfishness (*kelipot*) by continually unifying the many in the One through acts of selfless giving and embracing. In time the glittering shell of self (*kelipat nogah*) is consumed, and you know without doubt that you and all things are manifestions of God. This is why God is known as "a consuming fire" (Deuteronomy 4:24).

This is the hope of the inbetweener: to be consumed by the fire of God; to be embraced by the infinite love of the One who is all. For the righteous (*tzaddik*), such hope is unnecessary, for they are always on fire with God's love. For the wicked (*rasha*), such hope is meaningless, for they are devoted to remaining separate from God and godliness. Only to the *beinoni*, the inbetweener, does such hope speak, for her's is a life of yearning channeled through the discipline of the spirit. If you wish to take up the path of the inbetweener, know you are taking up a great work, a work upon which the well-being of all worlds depends.

53 □ The One Is within You

God dwelt among us
in the Ten Commandments,
as it is written,
"The writing is the writing of God."[1, 2]

When the Tablets were lost,
the *Shechinah* wandered,
and in time came to dwell
in the way of practice.[3]
This is why when you study Torah,
"the *Shechinah* is with you."[4]
But this is true only
if study leads to action,
for even the brightest flame requires oil.[5]
The flame of God is fed
by the oil of love and kindness.[6]

Shechinah is the flame,
your body the wick,
and your deeds the oil.
Just as the flame consumes the wick,
so *Shechinah* consumes the
illusion of otherness.
This is what is meant by the verse
"For *YHVH* your God is a consuming fire."[7, 8]

Notes ☐

Introduction

1. While usually rendered Habad or Chabad, I capitalize the consonants of the word to highlight the fact that it is an acronym for *CHochmah*, *Binah*, and *Da'at*—wisdom, rational understanding, and the integrative knowledge that arises when the first informs the second.

2. Shalom DovBer, Avtzon, *The Tanya, Its Story and History* (Brooklyn: Rabbi Shalom DovBer Avtzon, 1999), p. 4.

3. Hillel Levine, *Politics and Spirituality in Early Modern Jewish Messianism* (Jerusalem: Studies in Jewish Thought, 2001), pp. 16–17.

4. *Tikkunei Zohar*, *Tikkun* 57, p. 91b.

Key Philosophical Ideas

1. Martin Buber, *Ten Rungs: Collected Hasidic Sayings* (Secaucus, NJ: Citadel Press, 1995), p. 69.

Core Spiritual Practices

1. Mark Zborowski and Elizabeth Herzog, *Life Is with People: The Culture of the Shtetl* (New York: Schocken Books, 1952), pp. 193–94.

2. Maimonides, *Mishneh Torah*, *Hilchot Matanot Aniyim* 10:1, 10:7–14.

Glossary of Hebrew Terms ☐

Adam Kadmon: "Primordial Human." The first and most inclusive of the five worlds of divine emanation, *Adam Kadmon* and its accompanying intelligence *Yechidah* reveal the nonduality of God in, with, and as all reality.

Ahavah: Love, one of the two primal emotions (the other being fear) known to *Ruach*, the emotional intelligence operating on the level of *Yetzirah*.

Ahavah rabbah: God's infinite love for all reality.

Ahavat olam: The love of the world that arises when you realize God fills all reality.

Amidah: Literally "Standing Prayer." Liturgical benedictions recited during every prayer service.

Assiyah: The fifth and least inclusive world of the five worlds of divine emanation, *Assiyah* and its accompanying intelligence *Nefesh* reveal the physical dimension of reality.

Assur: Prohibited actions.

Atzilut: The second of the five worlds of divine emanation, *Atzilut* and its accompanying intelligence *Chayyah* reveal the social or interdependent aspect of reality.

Atzvut: The debilitating sense of alienation and despair that arises when you feel completely cut off from and incapable of realizing your union with God.

Ayn: God as emptiness, lacking all form.

Ayn Sof: God as the Infinite, that which is without (*ayn*) end (*sof*).

Beinoni: The inbetweener, those spiritual seekers who are neither saints nor sociopaths.

Beriah: The third of the five worlds of divine emanation, *Beriah* and its accompanying intelligence *Neshamah* reveal the egoic or independent aspect of reality.

Binah: The second of the Three Mothers, the three aspects of *Neshamah's* intellect, *Binah* is the capacity for rational understanding.

Bittul, bittul hayesh: The annihilation of all form and sense of separate identity.

B'nei aliyah: "Those who ascend," referring to those saints who can trace the source of evil back to its root in goodness, and in so doing transform evil into good.

Chayyah*:* Social or spiritual intelligence revealing the interdependence of all things.

Chesed*:* Kindness; the fourth *sefirah* of the kabbalistic Tree of Life.

Choch*:* Suchness, the essential nature of things.

Chochmah*:* Intuitive wisdom, the first of the Three Mothers, the three aspects of the intellect.

Da'at*:* Integrative knowledge, the third of the Three Mothers, the three aspects of the intellect.

Da'at devekut*:* The realization that all things are aspects of the one "Thing," God.

Drash*:* To investigate; the third hermeneutical level of reading Torah.

Elohim*:* God (literally "gods"), referring to that aspect of divinity that manifests in and as *Yesh*, seemingly separate forms.

Emunah*:* Literally "faith," but taken in *Tanya* to mean spiritual discipline.

Gadlut*:* Spaciousness, referring to the ability of the awakened mind to hold all things while identifying with none.

Gehinnom*:* Hell, a sense of extreme alienation from God and creation.

Gevurah*:* Strength; the fifth *sefirah* of the kabbalistic Tree of Life.

Halachah*:* From *halach*, "to walk," referring to the body of Jewish law for walking rightly in the world.

Hishtalshelut*:* The "chain" of divine emanations from the most to the least inclusive.

Hod*:* Glory, surrender; the eighth *sefirah* of the kabbalistic Tree of Life.

Kareit*:* The sense of being "cut off," from God and community.

Kavanah*:* The conscious "intention" to act in a manner that reveals the unity of God, woman, man, and nature.

Kelim*:* The containers originally designed to hold the creative energy of God.

Kelipat nogah*:* The "glittering shell" of egoic selfhood.

Kelipot*:* Plural of *kelipah*, "shell," the boundary that allows things to function with a sense of self.

Kesef hakodashim*:* A "longing for holy things" and for God.

Klot hanefesh*:* The desire of the self for complete emptying into God.

Lishmah*:* Doing something "for its own sake," without any ulterior motive.

Maasim tovim*:* "Good deeds," those random acts of kindness that one performs *lishmah*.

Mah*:* "What is," reality.

Makkif*:* "Surrounding," referring to the Presence of God that surrounds and permeates all reality.

Malchut*:* Kingship; the tenth *sefirah* of the kabbalistic Tree of Life.

Matrunita: Aramaic for "Queen," another word for the Presence of God manifest in and as the material world.

Memale kol almin: Aramaic for "the immanent light," the light of God present in all things.

Middot: The "character traits" one is to cultivate to realize the Presence of God.

Mitzvah (pl. *mitzvot*): Divine commands designed to awaken one to the Presence of God.

Mitzvah stam: The "quintessential *mitzvah*," referring to *tzedakah*, acts of economic justice and generosity.

Mitzrayim: Literally "Egypt," but used in *Tanya* as a pun for *m'tzar'im,* "from the narrows." *Mitzrayim* refers to all those places the ego is enslaved to narrowness and selfishness.

Muttar: Permitted actions.

Nefesh: Physical intelligence governing the workings of living beings.

Neshamah: Egoic intelligence revealing the independence of all things.

Netzach: Victory, determination; the seventh *sefirah* of the kabbalistic Tree of Life.

Penimiyut: The divine essence that is the innermost nature of all things.

Peshat: Simple; the first and literal level of reading Torah.

Rasha: A sociopath, one of the three types of people mentioned in the *Tanya.*

Ratzo: The desire to "run" toward self-annihilation in God, the way a moth flies into a flame.

Remez: Hint; the second or allegorical level of reading Torah.

Ruach: Emotional intelligence governing the primal feelings of love and fear.

Ruach HaKodesh: Holy Spirit; the capacity to intuit the unity of God in which and as all things.

Sefirot: The ten branches of the Tree of Life (*Etz Chayyim*): Keter (crown of infinite light), *Chochmah* (wisdom), *Binah* (understanding), *Chesed* (kindness), *Gevurah* (strength), *Tiferet* (beauty, balance), *Netzach* (victory, determination), *Hod* (glory, surrender), *Yesod* (foundation, will), and *Malchut* (kingship, realization of the divine plan in which all beings are aware of themselves as a part of rather than apart from God).

Seichel: The "intellect," referring to the three highest faculties of *Neshamah* (egoic) intelligence: *Chochmah, Binah,* and *Da'at.*

Shechinah: The Presence of God in and around all things.

Shevirat kelim: Shattering of the vessels; refers to the teaching of Rabbi Isaac Luria regarding the creation of the world. God's intent was to create a world without evil by carefully pouring divine energy into vessels *(kelim)* constructed to hold it. The vessels shattered, allowing for a broken universe in which evil can take root.

Shlemut: The nonduality of God.

Sh'ma: The fundamental affirmation of Judaism: "Hear (*sh'ma*), O Israel, *YHVH* is God, *YHVH* is One."

Shov: The balancing desire of *ratzo* (run), *shov* is the desire to "return" to the world of seeming separate forms to illumine the darkness of ignorance with the light of divine love.

Sitra achra: The "other side" of reality focused on separateness, independence, scarcity, and alienation from God and nature.

Sod: Secret; the fourth or mystical level of reading Torah.

Sovev kol almin: Aramaic for "the encompassing light," referring to the light of God surrounding all things.

Tanna: Teacher; refers to the rabbinic scholars of the Oral Law who lived in the last years of the first century BCE to the middle years of the second century CE. The teachings of the *Tannaim* (plural) are found in the Mishnah.

Teshuvah: Return; the act of repentance that returns you to your true nature as the image and likeness of God.

Tevunah: "Comprehension," the awareness of God's infinity permeating all reality.

Tiferet: Beauty, balance; the sixth *sefirah* of the kabbalistic Tree of Life.

Timtum halev: The "dullness of heart" that leaves one completely without motivation.

Torah lishmah: Torah for its own sake; the act of studying Torah without any ulterior motive.

Tzaddik (pl. *tzaddikim*): A saint, one of the three personality types found in *Tanya*.

Tzedakah: From *tzedek*, "justice," referring to the category of *mitzvot* (commandments) dealing with economic justice and financial generosity.

Tzimtzum: The act of divine "contraction" that gives rise to the illusion of divine separation.

Yechidah: Nondual intelligence revealing all things to be variations of the One Thing, God.

Yesh: Literally, "there is," referring to the seemingly separate forms of being.

Yesod: Foundation, will; the ninth *sefirah* of the kabbalistic Tree of Life.

Yetzer hara: The "evil inclination," the egoic impulse for self-focus and self-preservation that becomes "evil" when used to promote and excuse selfishness and exploitation of others.

Yetzer hatov: The "good inclination," the egoic impulse to care for others.

Yetzirah: The fourth of the five worlds of divine emanation, *Yetzirah* and its accompanying intelligence *Ruach* govern the instinctual and primal emotional aspects of living beings.

YHVH: The ineffable four-letter Name of God. A variation on the Hebrew verb "to be," *YHVH* is the dynamic creation, destruction, and re-creation of all reality.

Yichud elyon: The "higher unification," referring to the ecstatic melting of the self into God.

Yirah: Meaning both "fear" and "awe," *yirah* is one of the two primal emotions (the other being love) known to *Ruach*, the emotional intelligence operating on the level of *Yetzirah*.

Yirah ila'ah: "Higher awe," the level of awe that arises when you realize the infinite nature of God's redemptive love that is ready to embrace you regardless of how far you have fallen.

Yirah tata'ah: "Lower awe," the level of fear that arises when you realize how far your life is from the spiritual ideal of love.

Books Cited in *Tanya* □

Bava Batra ("Last Gate"): The third tractate of the order *Nezikin* in the Mishnah. *Bava Batra* deals with laws pertaining to real estate, inheritance, deeds, and legal documents.

Bava Metzia ("First Gate"): The first tractate of the order *Nezikin* in the Mishnah, *Bava Metzia* deals with laws pertaining to damages and compensation.

Berachot ("Benedictions"): The first tractate of the order *Zera'im* in the Mishnah, *Berachot* deals with the recitation of the *Sh'ma*, *Amidah*, and other prayers and blessings.

Deuteronomy: The fifth book of the Five Books of Moses (Torah). Called *Devarim* ("Words") in Hebrew, Deuteronomy is a retelling of the major narrative and laws of the previous four books of the Torah. Current scholarship places the writing of Deuteronomy sometime during the seventh century BCE.

Ecclesiastes (*Kohelet*, "Preacher"): A book of skeptical philosophy traditionally ascribed to King Solomon. Part of the biblical wisdom literature, Ecclesiastes was most likely written in the late third century BCE.

Exodus (*Shemot*, "Names"): The second of the Five Books of Moses (Torah), Exodus continues the biblical narrative from the death of Joseph to the liberation of the Hebrew people from Egypt and their wandering in the desert.

Genesis (*Bereshit*, "In the Beginning"): The first of the Five Books of Moses (Torah), Genesis tells the story of early humanity before focusing on Abraham, Sarah, and their descendants, ending with the migration of the Hebrew people into Egypt during a great famine.

Hilchot Shabbat: Laws of the Sabbath; part of Maimonides' *Mishneh Torah*, a summation of Jewish law written in the twelfth century.

Hilchot Yesodei HaTorah: Foundational Laws of Torah; part of Maimonides' *Mishneh Torah*, a summation of Jewish law written in the twelfth century. *Hilchot Yesodei HaTorah* deals with ten essential Jewish laws: 1) to recognize God; 2) to refrain from speculating on gods other than God; 3) to unify God; 4) to love God; 5) to fear God; 6) to sanctify God's Name; 7) to refrain from desecrating God's Name; 8) to refrain from destroying anything on which is written God's Name; 9) to listen to prophets who speak in God's Name; and 10) to refrain from testing God.

Hilchot Yom Tov: Laws Pertaining to the Holy Days; part of Maimonides' *Mishneh Torah*, a summation of Jewish law written in the twelfth century.

Hosea: The first book of the Twelve Minor Prophets. Hosea prophesied in Israel from 769 to 698 BCE.

Isaiah: The first book of the Major Prophets. Isaiah prophesied during the late eighth century BCE.

Jeremiah: The second book of the Major Prophets. Jeremiah prophesied from 626 to 580 BCE.

Jerusalem Talmud (*Talmud Yerushalmi*, also called the Palestinian Talmud): The older and smaller of the two Talmuds. Despite its name, the Jerusalem Talmud was compiled in the Galilee in the latter half of the fourth century CE, about two hundred years prior to the larger Babylonian Talmud.

Job: Written no later than the sixth century BCE, the Book of Job is a profound poetic examination of the problem of evil and suffering.

Kiddushin ("Sanctification"): The seventh tractate of the order *Nashim* ("Women") in the Mishnah, *Kiddushin* deals with issues pertaining to betrothal and marriage.

Leviticus (*Vayikra*, "And He Called"): The third of the Five Books of Moses (Torah), Leviticus focuses primarily on the rules associated with Levitical priesthood.

Makkot ("Lashes"): The fifth tractate of the order *Nezikin* in the Mishnah, *Makkot* deals with matters of criminal justice in the cases of crimes punishable by flogging.

Malachi: The last book of the Twelve Minor Prophets. The title may refer to the name of a specific prophet who lived in the mid-fifth century BCE or may be a title, "My Messenger."

Megillah ("Scroll"): The tenth tractate of the order *Mo'ed* in the Mishnah, *Megillah* deals primarily with the laws relating to the reading of the Scroll of Esther on Purim.

Midrash Tanchuma: A fifth-century collection of commentary ascribed to Rabbi Tanchuma, a Talmudic sage, but probably written centuries later.

Mishnah: Oral teaching; the earliest anthology of rabbinic teaching. Codified by Judah haNasi around the year 200 CE, the Mishnah contains teachings of the *Tannaim*, the first five generations of rabbinic sages beginning in the first century BCE, and their immediate predecessors.

Mishneh Torah: Literally "Repetition of the Torah"; completed around 1185 CE, *Mishneh Torah* was Maimonides' synthesis of Jewish law. Focusing solely on the rulings and the principles underlying them, it avoids the detailed dialectic of rabbinic discourse, and offers the reader a simple code of Jewish practice.

Nedarim ("Vows"): The third tractate of the order *Nashim* in the Mishnah, *Nedarim* deals with vows dedicating oneself or one's property to God.

Numbers (*Bemidbar*, "In the Wilderness"): The fourth of the Five Books of Moses (Torah), Numbers continues the story of the Hebrews' wanderings in Sinai.

Pe'ah ("Corner" of the field): The second tractate of the order *Zera'im* in the Mishnah, *Pe'ah* deals with the obligations farmers have regarding the poor.

Pesachim ("Paschal Sacrifices"): The third tractate of the order *Mo'ed* of the Mishnah, *Pesachim* deals with the laws pertaining to *matzah* (unleavened bread) during the holy week of Pesach (Passover).

Pirke Avot ("Chapters of the Fathers"): The ninth tractate of the order *Nezikin* in the Mishnah, *Pirke Avot* is an anthology of rabbinic ethical teachings covering a period of five hundred years from 300 BCE to 200 CE.

Proverbs (*Mishlei*): Ascribed to King Solomon, but compiled over centuries and edited in the eighth century BCE, Proverbs is an anthology in the Bible of practical self-help teachings.

Psalms (*Tehillim*): A compilation of 150 hymns in the Bible ascribed to King David, but composed by many authors from 1100 BCE to 50 BCE.

2 Samuel: Continues the story of the eleventh-century-BCE Hebrew prophet Samuel. Originally First and Second Samuel were a single book in the original Hebrew Bible, but it was broken into two parts in the Greek Septuagint and the Latin Vulgate. This custom was incorporated into printed Hebrew Bibles in the sixteenth century.

Sanhedrin ("Courts"): The fourth tractate of the order *Nezikin* in the Mishnah, *Sanhedrin* deals with the laws pertaining to courts of law.

Shabbat ("Sabbath"): The first tractate of the order *Mo'ed* in the Mishnah, *Shabbat* deals with the laws pertaining to the observance of the Sabbath.

Shnei Luchot HaBrit ("Two Tablets of the Covenant"): A sixteenth-century kabbalistic text authored by Rabbi Isaiah ben Avraham HaLevi Horowitz (1565–1630).

Song of Songs (*Shir HaShirim*): An anthology in the Bible of Hebrew love songs ascribed to King Solomon and written sometime in the second century BCE.

Sotah ("Wife Suspected of Adultery"): The fifth tractate of the order *Nashim* in the Mishnah, *Sotah* refers to laws pertaining to a wife suspected of marital infidelity.

Talmud: From the Hebrew root *l-m-d*, to "study" or "teach," the definitive anthology of ancient rabbinic law compiled over a period of seven centuries (200 BCE–500 CE). The Talmud is composed of two separate works, the Mishnah, the earliest compilation of rabbinic teaching codified in the third century CE, and the Gemara, further rabbinic elaboration on the Mishnah. There are two Talmuds: the *Talmud Yerushalmi*, or Jerusalem Talmud (see Jerusalem Talmud), and the *Talmud Bavli*, or Babylonian Talmud. The *Bavli* is the larger and more inclusive work and usually takes precedence over the earlier and smaller *Yerushalmi*.

Tikkunei Zohar ("Chapters of the *Zohar*"): A fourteenth-century mystical text of unknown authorship, written in the style of the *Zohar*, and included as part of the *Zohar*, *Tikkunei Zohar* looks at more than seventy different interpretations of the word *bereshit*, "in the beginning."

Yoma ("Day"): The fifth tractate of the order *Mo'ed* in the Mishnah, *Yoma* deals with the role of the High Priest during Yom Kippur, the Day of Atonement.

Zephaniah: The ninth book of the Twelve Minor Prophets, Zephaniah focuses on three oracles by Zephaniah prophesied during the reign of King Josiah (639–609 BCE).

Zohar ("Book of Splendor"): A mystical commentary on Torah, *Zohar* is the central work of medieval Kabbalah. Ascribed to the first-century-BCE sage Rabbi Yochanan bar Yochai, the *Zohar* was most likely written by Rabbi Moses de Leon during the last decades of the thirteenth century in Castile, Spain.

Suggestions for Further Reading ☐

Avtzon, Sholom DovBer. *The Tanya, Its Story and History from Its Origins to Today*. Brooklyn: Avtzon, 1999.

Buber, Martin. *Hasidism*. New York: Philosophical Library, 1948.

———. *Hasidism and Modern Man*. New York: Prometheus Books, 1988.

———. *Origin and Meaning of Hasidism*. New York: Harper Torchbooks, 1960.

———. *The Way of Man: According to Hasidic Teaching*. Woodstock, VT: Jewish Lights, 2012.

Dan, Joseph. *The Teachings of Hasidism*. Springfield, NJ: Behrman House Publishing, 1996.

Ehrlich, Avrum. *The Messiah of Brooklyn: Understanding Lubavitch Hasidism Past and Present*. Jersey City, NJ: Ktav Publishing House, 2005.

Elior, Rachel. *The Mystical Origins of Hasidism*. Oxford: Littman Library of Jewish Civilization, 2008.

———. *The Paradoxical Ascent to God: The Kabbalistic Theosophy of Habad Hasidism*. Albany: SUNY Press, 1992.

Foxbrunner, Roman. *Habad: The Hasidism of R. Shneur Zalman of Lyady*. Lanham, MD: Jason Aronson, 1993.

Green, Arthur. *Ehyeh: A Kabbalah for Tomorrow*. Woodstock, VT: Jewish Lights, 2004.

———. *Judaism's Ten Best Ideas: A Brief Guide for Seekers*. Woodstock, VT: Jewish Lights, 2014.

Green, Yekutiel. *Commentary on the Tanya*. 2 vols. Kfar Chabad, 2005.

———. *Themes in Tanya*. Kfar Chabad, 1992.

Idel, Moshe. *Hasidism: Between Ecstasy and Magic*. Albany: SUNY Press, 2007.

Liadi, Schneur Zalman. *The Tanya: Bi-Lingual Edition*. Trans. Nissan Mindel. Brooklyn, NY: Kehot Publication Society, 1998.

Rabinowicz, Tzvi. *The Encyclopedia of Hasidism*. Lanham, MD: Jason Aronson, 1996.

Shapiro, Rami. *Amazing* Chesed: *Living a Grace-Filled Judaism*. Woodstock, VT: Jewish Lights, 2012.

———. *Ethics of the Sages:* Pirkei Avot—*Annotated & Explained*. Woodstock, VT: SkyLight Paths, 2006.

————. *Hasidic Tales: Annotated & Explained.* Woodstock, VT: SkyLight Paths, 2004.

————. *The Hebrew Prophets: Selections Annotated & Explained.* Woodstock, VT: SkyLight Paths, 2006.

————. *The Sacred Art of Lovingkindness: Preparing to Practice.* Woodstock, VT: SkyLight Paths, 2006.

Steinsaltz, Adin. *Learning From the Tanya.* San Francisco: Jossey-Bass, 2005.

————. *Opening The Sacred Art of the Tanya.* San Francisco: Jossey-Bass, 2003.

————. *The Thirteen Petalled Rose,* Rev. ed. San Francisco: Jossey-Bass, 2011.

————. *Understanding the Tanya.* San Francisco: Jossey-Bass, 2007.

Uffenheimer, Rivka. *Hasidism as Mysticism: Quietistic Elements in Eighteenth Century Hasidic Thought.* Princeton, NJ: Princeton University Press, 1993.

Wineberg, Yosef. *Lessons in Tanya.* 5 vols. Brooklyn: Kehot Publication Society, 1997.

About Jewish Lights

People of all faiths and backgrounds yearn for books that attract, engage, educate, and spiritually inspire.

Our principal goal is to stimulate thought and help all people learn about who the Jewish People are, where they come from, and what the future can be made to hold. While people of our diverse Jewish heritage are the primary audience, our books speak to people in the Christian world as well and will broaden their understanding of Judaism and the roots of their own faith.

We bring to you authors who are at the forefront of spiritual thought and experience. While each has something different to say, they all say it in a voice that you can hear.

Our books are designed to welcome you and then to engage, stimulate, and inspire. We judge our success not only by whether or not our books are beautiful and commercially successful, but by whether or not they make a difference in your life.

For your information and convenience, at the back of this book we have provided a list of other Jewish Lights books you might find interesting and useful. They cover all the categories of your life:

Bar/Bat Mitzvah	Life Cycle
Bible Study / Midrash	Meditation
Children's Books	Men's Interest
Congregation Resources	Parenting
Current Events / History	Prayer / Ritual / Sacred Practice
Ecology / Environment	Social Justice
Fiction: Mystery, Science Fiction	Spirituality
Grief / Healing	Theology / Philosophy
Holidays / Holy Days	Travel
Inspiration	Twelve Steps
Kabbalah / Mysticism / Enneagram	Women's Interest

About SKYLIGHT PATHS Publishing

SkyLight Paths Publishing is creating a place where people of different spiritual traditions come together for challenge and inspiration, a place where we can help each other understand the mystery that lies at the heart of our existence.

Through spirituality, our religious beliefs are increasingly becoming a part of our lives—rather than *apart* from our lives. While many of us may be more interested than ever in spiritual growth, we may be less firmly planted in traditional religion. Yet, we do want to deepen our relationship to the sacred, to learn from our own as well as from other faith traditions, and to practice in new ways.

SkyLight Paths sees both believers and seekers as a community that increasingly transcends traditional boundaries of religion and denomination—people wanting to learn from each other, *walking together, finding the way.*

For your information and convenience, at the back of this book we have provided a list of other SkyLight Paths books you might find interesting and useful. They cover the following subjects:

Buddhism / Zen	Global Spiritual	Monasticism
Catholicism	Perspectives	Mysticism
Children's Books	Gnosticism	Poetry
Christianity	Hinduism /	Prayer
Comparative	Vedanta	Religious Etiquette
Religion	Inspiration	Retirement
Current Events	Islam / Sufism	Spiritual Biography
Earth-Based	Judaism	Spiritual Direction
Spirituality	Kabbalah	Spirituality
Enneagram	Meditation	Women's Interest
	Midrash Fiction	Worship

CPSIA information can be obtained
at www.ICGtesting.com
Printed in the USA
BVHW031347011221
622965BV00002B/47